A PLUME BOOK

ZUBI!

achi (אחי): my bro
achoti (אחותי): my sis
manush (מנוש): pussy
shtrungul (שטרונגול): dick
tachat (תחת): ass
sababa (סבבה): cool

DANNY BEN ISRAEL was born in Israel, where he is widely known as a singer-songwriter and a comic. He has also worked as an author, journalist, and editor, writing in both Hebrew and English. Currently, Danny is touring with a show of Israeli and Jewish folklore. He splits his time between New York, Tel Aviv, and Vienna.

ZUBI!

The Real Hebrew You Were Never Taught in School

Danny Ben Israel

Illustrated by Chris Murphy

A PLUME BOOK

PLUME
Published by the Penguin Group
Penguin Group (USA) Inc., 375 Hudson Street, New York, New York 10014, U.S.A. •
Penguin Group (Canada), 90 Eglinton Avenue East, Suite 700, Toronto, Ontario, Canada
M4P 2Y3 (a division of Pearson Penguin Canada Inc.) • Penguin Books Ltd., 80 Strand,
London WC2R 0RL, England • Penguin Ireland, 25 St. Stephen's Green, Dublin 2,
Ireland (a division of Penguin Books Ltd.) • Penguin Group (Australia), 250 Camberwell
Road, Camberwell, Victoria 3124, Australia (a division of Pearson Australia Group Pty.
Ltd.) • Penguin Books India Pvt. Ltd., 11 Community Centre, Panchsheel Park, New
Delhi – 110 017, India • Penguin Group (NZ), 67 Apollo Drive, Rosedale, North Shore
0632, New Zealand (a division of Pearson New Zealand Ltd.) • Penguin Books (South
Africa) (Pty.) Ltd., 24 Sturdee Avenue, Rosebank, Johannesburg 2196, South Africa

Penguin Books Ltd., Registered Offices: 80 Strand, London WC2R 0RL, England

First published by Plume, a member of Penguin Group (USA) Inc.

First Printing, March 2011
10 9 8 7 6 5 4 3 2 1

Illustrations by Chris Murphy

 REGISTERED TRADEMARK—MARCA REGISTRADA

LIBRARY OF CONGRESS CATALOGING-IN-PUBLICATION DATA

Ben Israel, Dani.
 Zubi! : the real Hebrew you were never taught in school / Danny Ben Israel;
illustrated by Chris Murphy.
  p. cm.
 ISBN 978-0-452-29689-3 (pbk.: alk. paper) 1. Hebrew wit and humor. 2. Hebrew
Language—Terms and phrases. I. Title.
 PN6231.J5B355 2011
818'.602—dc22   2010037199

Printed in the United States of America

To my heroes:
W. C. Fields and Bugs Bunny

Contents

Acknowledgments

I want to thank the people who helped make this book happen: Noam (Norm) Niv, my first-ever editor, for his constant inspiration and support; Michal Daniel, my dearest one and only, was the person first approached about this book, for being too lazy and suggesting me instead; Al Zuckerman, the best literary agent one can wish for, for his generosity; Nancy Meyer for her dedication and for making my English sound less Israeli; Chris Murphy for his joyous drawings; and Nadia Kashper, my editor, for her magnificent magic touch.

Introduction

I should have been surprised when, by a freak coincidence, I was invited to write a book about Israeli slang. But I wasn't. It felt quite natural, like a logical extension of my career. I'm an Israeli folk singer. I don't sing *to* audiences; I sing with them. I take pleasure not so much in their applause as in the light of their shining eyes once I get them going. The rapport I enjoy with my audience has enabled me to learn new songs, jokes, and lots of slang, which I sometimes incorporate into my shows.

I'm fond of slang. It's divine and creative and, most of all, antiestablishment and delightfully anarchistic. It's the expression of a free human spirit. "Vox populi, vox Dei," says a famous Latin proverb: "The voice of the people is the voice of G-D." Isn't slang just that? Even G-D sometimes uses slang, as you'll see in chapter 4. Most of the words in our vocabulary were probably coined in an onomatopoeic or associative manner as the need arose. That doesn't mean every bit of slang is finally incorporated into the legitimate language. Some words are but passing fancies. The few that withstand the **shiney hazman** (שיני הזמן), or "teeth of time," tend to represent basic, unchangeable facts about the human condition.

Slang flourishes wherever gaps in the proper language need to be filled. It is a matter not only of words but how they're used—matter-of-factly. I could follow this train of thought to the point of claiming that slang is a way of life, and maybe even further than that. For now, I'll just say that for me the best slang is original, reflecting a truth that comes from within.

In this book I've tried to avoid words that might have a short life span. A lot of new slang loses its vitality after only a few months, or maybe a year at the most, especially when it becomes too popular too fast. Words make the rounds, and then—poof!—they're gone. That's not saying all my choices are evergreen—only time will tell—but some have already lasted thousands of years, and most should be good for a few more.

The book is divided into chapters, each with a short introduction and . . . yackety-yak . . . yak, yak . . . yak, yak (I always hate this part). I'm sure you'll get along fine without being told how to use the book. Don't bother memorizing all the words (anyhow, you won't be able to). If it's vocabulary you're after, at the very end of the book you'll find a list of terms in English alphabetical order.

Israel is a vibrant place. Its people take full advantage of life—every minute, every drop of it. If you consider the threats that Israel faces, you'll understand why living is such a highly cherished commodity.

There is another, more fundamental, reason for the Israeli obsession with life: Judaism arose as an antithesis to the ancient Egyptian obsession with death. It so happened that Moses woke up one morning in Pharaoh's palace, in a bad mood, saying to himself: "Fuck (**lezayen** לזיין) that shit (**chara** חרא) about everlasting life. I have yet to see anybody come back from the dead. Let's get out of this morbid graveyard and do some living." And since he was convinced that there was no right way of dying, he took his folks out of Egypt and gave them a doctrine for a right way of living—one pretty well summed up in this joke.

A patient goes to the doctor and tells him he is feeling very sick.

Doctor: Do you smoke?
Patient: No.
Doctor: Do you drink?
Patient: No.
Doctor: Do you have sex?
Patient: No.
Doctor: Then drop dead.

And here is how it looks and sounds in Hebrew. Remember, we read and write from right to left! (Don't get discouraged by the strange letters; once you're familiar with them you'll be able to recognize, if not each letter, for sure some words.)

Rofe: Ata meashen? (ד"ר: אתה מעשן?)
Chole: Lo. (חולה: לא.)
Rofe: Ata shote? (ד"ר: אתה שותה?)
Chole: Lo. (חולה: לא.)
Rofe: Ata mekayem maga-mini? (ד"ר: אתה מקיים מגע מיני?)
Chole: Lo. (חולה: לא.)
Rofe: Az lech tamut. (ד"ר: אז לך תמות.)

Use this book in good health!

ZUBI!

CHAPTER ONE

Zubi and Other Basics

Zubi

Even more than to teach you new words, I want this book to give you insight into the slangy side of the real Israel. That's why I've called it *Zubi!*

Zubi (זובי) is one of several Hebrew words that mean "penis." It's also used to express total defiance—a definite "No way!" that is characteristically Israeli. Without being able to say **zubi** stubbornly again and again, we, with our distinct language and culture, wouldn't have survived our past and present (and probably future) persecutions, and I wouldn't be sitting comfortably and securely in my Tel Aviv home, writing a book about Hebrew slang.

A big **zubi** to everything that keeps us apart from each other and from ourselves. **Zubi** to all those who try to impose on us things we don't need and don't want. Another **zubi** goes to all who think Israel is just a land of milk and honey and money.

The nice thing about **zubi** is that you don't need to add anything to it to emphasize your point or your determination—not even a syllable. It's the bottom line: *No!* And although it's indeed a name for the male organ, it's completely void of sexual con-notation, as you can see from this exchange between me and my friend Moshe.

I asked, "What does she want from you?"

He replied, "She wanted two things: a hard dick and money. A hard dick I've given her. Money? **Zubi** she'll get!"

Here is how this conversation sounds and looks in Hebrew (note that **zayin** זין is the standard word for a penis):

> **Ani:** Ma hi rotza mimcha?
>
> (אני: מה היא רוצה ממך?)
>
> **Moshe:** Shney dvarim hi ratzta: zayin kashe vekesef. Zayin kashe natati la. Kesef? Zubi hi tkabel!
>
> (משה: שני דברים היא רצתה: זין קשה וכסף. זין קשה נתתי לה, כסף? זובי תקבל!)

The gist of **zubi** can also be expressed by bending your elbow at a forty-five-degree angle, with your hand held palm up, stretched out, and swishing from side to side. This hand ges-ture is a way of silently saying **zubi** with a vengeance. It means, "I'm on to you and won't let it happen. Do you want to make something out of it?" Next time it seems like a taxi driver is taking you for a ride, try it. He'll understand that you mean **Rak biglal sheani tayar ata choshev shetuchal la-avod alay?** (רק בגלל שאני תייר אתה חושב שתוכל לעבוד עלי?): "Just because I'm a tourist do you think you can take me for a ride?" Since this ges-ture carries a threat of retaliation, be careful how you use it and make sure you can back it up.

Be aware that the gesture has a completely different meaning if you move the palm only once. It becomes the familiar, harmless question mark gesture meaning "What?" or "Where?" or "Why?"

While we're on the topic of hand gestures: in Israel one gives the finger in the traditional Middle Eastern way. With the hand held vertically, the middle finger is bent in toward the palm, while the rest of the fingers are kept straight. This gesture is dynamic, unlike its immobile American cousin; you point your finger at the one you wish would go fuck himself, and then move it suggestively up and down.

To do and make

There is a lot of action in Israel, a lot of hustle and bustle. People are industrious, always busy, always running. No wonder, then, that one of the words most commonly used by Israelis is the verb **la-asot** (לעשות). It means both "to do" and "to make." In this case, Hebrew doesn't split hairs like English.

Indeed, in Hebrew, **la-asot** is unorthodoxly applied to almost any activity for which you don't have the patience to think of the right verb. You'll find it very useful once you get the hang of it.

Jews have always been fond of this word. It is interesting to note that when Moses read G-D's words to the Israelites for the first time, in the Sinai desert, their immediate reaction was, "We will do and hear" (Exodus 24:7). The interpretive translation in the King James Bible reads, "We will do and be obedient." Doing is very important in Judaism, and **la-asot** comes in very handy in Israel today.

The declensions are:

Masculine, Feminine

Present

singular (the same for first, second, and third person)

ose (עושה), **osa** (עושה)

plural

osim (עושים), **osot** (עושות)

PAST

singular

1p.) **asiti** (עשיתי), **asiti** (עשיתי)

2p.) **asita** (עשית), **asit** (עשית)

3p.) **asa** (עשה), **asta** (עשתה)

plural

1p.) **asinu** (עשינו), **asinu** (עשינו)

2p.) **asitem** (עשיתם), **asiten** (עשיתן)

3p.) **asu** (עשו), **asu** (עשו)

FUTURE

singular

1p.) **e-ese** (אעשה), **e-ese** (אעשה)

2p.) **ta-ase** (תעשה), **ta-asi** (תעשי)

3p.) **ya-ase** (יעשה), **ta-ase** (תעשה)

plural

1p.) **na-ase** (נעשה), **na-ase** (נעשה)

2p.) **ta-asu** (תעשו), **ta-asu** (תעשו)

3p.) **ya-asu** (יעשו), **ta-asena** (תעשינה)

La-asot beyt sefer.

Here are a few examples of how the verb is used:

la-asot kavod (לעשות כבוד): to show respect; literally, "to make honor"

la-asot bushot (לעשות בושות): to behave in a shameful way; literally, "to do shame"

la-asot guf (לעשות גוף): to flex one's muscles; literally, "to make a body"

la-asot et hamavet (לעשות את המוות): to give hell; literally, "to make death"

la-asot chayim (לעשות חיים): to have a great time; literally, "to make life"

la-asot bayad (לעשות ביד): to masturbate; literally, "to do in the hand"

la-asot cheshbon (לעשות חשבון): to show respect, to take into consideration, to humble oneself before someone or something bigger; literally, "to do the math"

la-asot ru-ach (לעשות רוח): to show off without any substance; literally, "to make wind"

la-asot beyt sefer (לעשות בית ספר): to teach someone a lesson; literally, "to make school"

la-asot tsava (לעשות צבא): to serve in the army; literally, "to do army"

la-asot shuk (לעשות שוק): to shop in a grocery store or buy food anywhere; literally, "to make market"

You'll see more phrases with this verb throughout the book.

Hell, devil, goats, and dogs

There is no mention of the devil in the Jewish Bible (which accounts for the lack of morbidity and fear of demons or sin in Israeli society), so there is really no Hebrew equivalent for "go to hell." But if you insist on sending someone there, you have two choices. One is **lech la-azazel** (לך לעזאזל), "go to Azazel," the biblical Azazel being a place in the desert to which a goat was sent on Yom Kippur to atone for the sins of the Israelites (thus the term "scapegoat"). You can also say **lech leaza** (לך לעזה), "go to Aza." Aza is not only an abbreviation of Azazel; it's also the Hebrew name for the city of Gaza, which—take it from one who has been there—is as close to hell as you can get.

There is another way to send someone to hell, but it's rarely used these days: **Halevay she-tamut bakever shell Hitler** (הלוואי שתמות בקבר של היטלר), or "May you die in Hitler's grave."

Ancient Hebrew does have a nickname for the devil, but most Israelis don't know about it. So I'll enlighten you. One phrase we use freely is **lizrok etsem** (לזרוק עצם), "to throw a bone." For instance, when we think a friendly stock market trader has some insider information, we'll say **zrok etsem** (זרוק עצם), "throw us a bone."

This phrase is part of a larger and older one, **lizrok etsem lakelev** (לזרוק עצם לכלב), which means "to throw a bone at the dog." Although these words are commonly used, very few Israelis know their origin and true meaning.

The phrase comes from the kabbalah, or Jewish mysticism, where Satan is depicted as a big black dog that can be appeased by being tossed a bone—not a juicy T-bone steak, mind you, but only a meatless bone with no real substance.

Some of you may wonder, why a dog? Why not a ferocious horned beast? The answer is simple. The fallen angel has no power

Lizrok etsem lakelev.

over us without explicit consent given of our free will. That's the nature of his mandate: he can't force himself on people, though he sure can seduce and trick. A ferocious beast would scare people away, but a pooch—man's best friend—is a different matter. We pat, feed, play, trust—the better to be lured in.

The verb "to throw" is very important in this case and was probably carefully chosen. You don't *offer* the bone to the dog, and you don't *give* it to him; you throw it at him from afar, as if chasing him away with a stone. By no means are you supposed to establish contact.

Let me illustrate this clearly. Say you unintentionally catch

a glimpse of your best friend's wife's cleavage when she inno-
cently bends down to pour you coffee. No big deal. You didn't
initiate it; it just happened. So you consider it a bone and throw
it to the dog. That means you throw away the sight of that cleavage and don't, for instance, start wondering how to get your best
friend's wife between the sheets. If you even contemplate such
a thing, it's no longer a bone. It has substance. It's already a sin
that won't wash away.

In the same vein, you can see that a "son of a bitch" isn't the
same in Hebrew as in English—the mother is the devil himself.

Here are some words and phrases that carry similar connotations:

kelev (כלב): dog

ben kalba (בן כלבה): son of a bitch

kelev ben kelev (כלב בן כלב): dog, son of a dog

haklavim novchim ach hashayara overet
(הכלבים נובחים אך השיירה עוברת): A wartime phrase meaning
"let the dogs bark at you and don't fret, just carry on with
your mission." I might say, for example, **Hamevakrim lo
ahavu et ha-albom hachron sheli; eyn davar, haklavim
novchim ach hashayara overet**
(לא אהבו את האלבום האחרון שלי; אין דבר, הכלבים נובחים אך השיירה עוברת
המבקרים): "The critics didn't like my last album; never mind,
the dogs bark but the caravan moves on."

lizrok laklavim (לזרוק לכלבים): to throw (someone) to the
dogs

mitkalev (מתכלב): Dogging. This term is used by Israeli
backpackers who roam the world after completing their
military service and before handing themselves over to the
daily grind. Dogging is living as cheaply as possible, even if

it means scavenging and sleeping in the gutter. So it's pretty close to hell.

Two Israeli backpackers meet on the main street of Manali, India, a favorite backpacking destination:

A: Hey, achi, matsati hostel zol, rak esrim rupi, ata ba?

(היי אחי, מצאתי הוסטל זול, רק עשרים רופי, אתה בא?)

B: Lo, ach sheli, yesh li od shlosha chodashim letayel, ani chayav lehitkalev.

(לא, אח שלי, יש לי עוד שלושה חודשים לטייל, אני חייב להתכלב.)

That is:

A: Hey, bro, I found a cheap hostel, only twenty rupees. Are you coming?

B: No, my brother, I still have three months to travel. I have to dog it out.

kelev sha-ashuim (כלב שעשועים): fun dog, someone to toy with

kol kelev ba yomo (כל כלב בא יומו): every dog has his day

lehair klavim merivtsam (להעיר כלבים מרבצם): to awaken sleeping dogs; similar to "let sleeping dogs lie"

zanav beyn haraglayim (זנב בין הרגליים): tail between the legs

adif kelev chaver mechaver kelev (עדיף כלב חבר מחבר כלב): better to have a dog as a friend than a friend who's a dog

po kavur hakelev (פה קבור הכלב): here is where the dog is buried; meaning this is where the problem lies

pudel (פודל): poodle, meaning a person who is someone's pet

kor klavim (קור כלבים): dog cold, meaning an evil cold that penetrates your bones

aruchat boker shel kelev (ארוחת בוקר של כלב): A dog's breakfast. Usually used to criticize, not a lousy breakfast, but rather a lousy person or object. As in **Tiree et habachura hazu, guf ptsatsa aval panim kmo aruchat boker shel kelev** (תראה את הבחורה הזו, גוף פצצה, אבל פנים כמו ארוחת בוקר של כלב): "Look at that girl. Her body is slammin', but her face is like a dog's breakfast."

Israelis acknowledge that there are demons, but we don't make a big fuss about them. We accept them as part of creation. Their duty is to scare and deter; our duty is to live and prosper in spite of them. Leave your demons behind when going to Israel or, better yet, bring them along. You might be able to chase them away or at least come to terms with them.

As the old Israeli proverb says, "The demon isn't that horrible" (**Hashed lo nora kol kach** השד לא נורא כל כך).

CHAPTER TWO

Practical Hebrew and Useful Slang You Already Know

Israelis are accustomed to trying to understand people who don't speak their language. The country is a land of immigrants, some of whom never learn Hebrew properly yet get along very well by following a few simple rules that will also work for you.

First, get to the point immediately. Say you need help finding an address. Don't start in with, "Excuse me, sir, would you please be so kind as to tell me how to get to . . ." If the person you approach is polite, they might endure the whole sentence; more likely, they'll walk away. Just say the name of the street you're looking for, with a questioning tone in your voice, and make the question mark hand gesture I mentioned in chapter 1. People will be grateful to you for not wasting their time.

To find the central bus station:

Tachana merkazit? (?תחנה מרכזית): Central station?

Catching a train:

Tachanat rakevet? (?תחנת רכבת): Train station?

It's even simpler to get to the airport (**sade teufa** שדה תעופה; literally, "field flight"). Just say **sade** to your cab driver.

If you need something at your hotel or hostel (or anywhere else in Israel), one word will usually suffice. If you want it in a hurry, all you need to do is add emphasis to your tone.

Magevet! (!מגבת): Towel!

Matsaim! (!מצעים): Bedclothes!

Sabon! (!סבון): Soup!

Cheshbon! (!חשבון): Bill!

Here are a few more essential words:

ken (כן): yes

lo (לא): no

beseder (בסדר): okay

ulay (אולי): maybe

tov (טוב): good

ra (רע): bad

kacha-kacha (ככה ככה): so-so

yafe (יפה): nice

mechoar (מכוער): ugly (for both people and objects)

achshav (עכשיו): now

yoter meuchar (יותר מאוחר): later

af pa-am (אף פעם): never

maher (מהר): fast

leat (לאט): slowly

yoter (יותר): more

pachot (פחות): less

day (די): enough

bediyuk (בדיוק): exactly

ir (עיר): town

rechov (רחוב): street

malon (מלון): hotel

bayit (בית): house

beyt shimush (בית שימוש): toilet

beyt zonot (בית זונות): whorehouse

beyt mirkachat (בית מרקחת): pharmacy; literally, "house of concoctions"

beyt cholim (בית חולים): hospital

rofe (רופא): physician

koev (כואב): hurts

chole (חולה): sick

bari (בריא): healthy

misada (מסעדה): restaurant

ochel (אוכל): food

mashkaot (משקאות): beverages

raev (רעב): hungry

savea (שבע): full (of food)

tsame (צמא): thirsty

shikor (שיכור): drunk

ayef (עייף): tired

lishon (לישון): to sleep

hashkama (השכמה): wake up

kesef (כסף): money

Kama? (כמה?): How much?

yoter miday (יותר מדי): too much

pachot miday (פחות מדי): too little

rotse (רוצה): to want

lo rotse (לא רוצה): don't want

mishtara (משטרה): police

Hatsilu! (הצילו!): Help! Literally, "Save me!"

ohev (אוהב): to love

sone (שונא): to hate

cham (חם): hot

kar (קר): cold

posher (פושר): lukewarm

When introducing yourself, it's common to point to yourself and say your name. Here are a couple of phrases that will come in handy when meeting people (I'll cover slang greetings in the next chapter).

Eych kor-im lecha? (איך קוראים לך?): What's your name?

naim meod (נעים מאוד): pleased to meet you; literally, "very pleasant"

To ask for someone's phone number, point at them and say, meaningfully, **telefon** (טלפון), "telephone." You can also use either of the following phrases:

Tavi telefon! (תביא טלפון!): Give (literally, "bring") telephone!

Ma hamispar shelcha? (מה המספר שלך?): What's your number?

After giving your digits, you can say:

titkasher (תתקשר): call me; literally, "get in touch"

Useful slang you already know

I warned you in the introduction that it would be difficult to remember all these words, but here's some nice news. You probably already speak a lot of the latest Israeli slang, much of which consists of words taken as is, or slightly adapted, from American music, movies, and TV shows.

You won't find most of these words in the Hebrew dictionary—yet. Maybe in a few generations. Use them as you would in English.

ace (אס)

baby (ביבי): used as a term of endearment

bitchit (ביצ׳ית): bitch

boss (בוס)

bug (באג): computer bug

bullshit (בולשיט)

buzz (באז): as in hype

bye (בי)

celeb (סלב)

chance (צ׳אנס)

comeback (קמבאק)

    lehitkambek (להתקמבק): to make a comeback

cool (קול)

copy (קופי)

duh (דא)

darling (דרלינג)

date (דייט)

deal (דיל)

DJ (דיג׳יי)

ecshen (אקשן): action. You might say, **Im ata rotse litpos ziyun, lech lemoadon hadom biymey chamishi, yesh sham harbe ecshen** (אם אתה רוצה לתפוש זיון לך למועדון הדום, יש שם הרבה אקשן): "If you want to get laid, go to the Dome club on Thursdays; there is a lot of action there."

ex (אקס)

fair (פייר)

fancy (פנסי)

fantasti (פנטסטי): fantastic

flop (פלופ)

freak (פריק)

fak (פאק): fuck

> **Fak! Shachachti lakachat kesef** (פאק! שכחתי לקחת כסף.):
> Fuck! I forgot to bring money. Or **Eyze fak! Shachachti
> lakachat kesef** (איזה פאק! שכחתי לקחת כסף.): What a fuck! I
> forgot to bring money.

fenomen (פנומן): phenomenon

> **fenomenali** (פנומנלי): phenomenal person

fun (פאן)

gay (גיי)

groggy (גרוגי)

hello (הלו)

hi (היי)

icon (אייקון)

in (אין)

job (ג'וב)

joint (ג'וינט)

junk (ג'אנק): as in useless stuff, not drugs

king (קינג)

larj (לארג'): large; typically used to describe a generous person

> **Hachaver sheli hu larj—hu tamid mazmin et kulam lemashke** (החבר שלי הוא לארג'. הוא תמיד מזמין את כולם למשקה): My friend is large—he always buys drinks for everyone.

look (לוק): as in fashion

loser (לוסר)

mommy (מאמי)

mega (מגה)

a must (מאסט)

no way (נו ווי)

never (נבר)

out (אאוט): as in outdated or out of fashion

outsider (אאוטסיידר)

over (אובר): used to amplify, as in

> **Ani over ayef** (אני אובר עייף): I'm overtired.

okay (או קיי)

perfect (פרפקט)

please (פליז)

push (פוש): as in pushing drugs

> **pusher** (פושר)

quickie (קוויקי)

rock 'n' roll (רוק'נרול)

shit (שיט)

> **Shit! Havisa sheli pag tokpa** (שיט! הוויזה שלי פג תוקפה.):
> Shit! My visa ran out.

shock (שוק)

shopping (שופינג)

snob (סנוב)

sorry (סורי)

style (סטייל)

switch (סוויץ): as in an on/off switch

touch ('טאץ): as in emotionally

trend (טראנד)

trip (טריפ)

ultimativi (אולטימטיבי): ultimate

underdog (אנדרדוג)

wow (וואו)

winner (וינר)

yeah (יה)

yes (יס)

Flow

You'll get along fine in Israel if you remember one essential word: **lizrom** (לזרום), "to flow," as in "to go with the flow."

By saying **lizrom**, you're actually saying, "Come on, bro, get with it! Just flow with the situation." You may find it useful in overcoming your own or someone else's hang-ups, like when you manage to get into bed on a first date and she, he, or it hesitates to go all the way. Just say, **tizremi chamuda, tizremi** (תזרמי חמודה תזרמי), "Flow, baby, flow." It might help.

If that doesn't keep things moving, you might try **Al tihiye kol kach kaved** (אל תהייה כל כך כבד): "Don't be so heavy."

CHAPTER THREE

Greeting People and Getting Rid of Them

Hi, brother

Israel is by no means a third world country. Its sticky familiarity only makes it appear that way. There are no formalities or social boundaries. Don't be surprised if complete strangers walk up to you and start intimate conversations as if you were old army buddies.

The ruling slang words for addressing people in Israel are:

achi (אחי): my brother, equivalent to "bro" and "dude"

achoti (אחותי): my sister

Achi and **achoti** originated as terms of camaraderie among soldiers during the 1982 Lebanon War. Their use is now widespread, especially among youngsters, and they're probably here to stay. They create instant familiarity and open paths to intimacy.

The other day I was walking my old **tarante** (טרנטה), a word that can be used for anything decrepit or falling apart—in this case my barely living dog. A car stopped beside me, and the driver asked, **Achi, ben kama hakelev?** (אחי, בן כמה הכלב?), "Hi brother, how old is the dog?" When I told him my dog was fourteen, he smiled at me and said, **Haya li kaze kelev, hirdamti oto lifney shvuayim** (היה לי כלב כזה הרדמתי אותו לפני שבועיים), "I had the same dog. I put him to sleep two weeks ago." In his eyes I saw the inevitable.

But that wasn't as bad as a few days later, when a young fellow drove by me and said, **Achi, ata lo choshev shehigia zman lehardim et hakelev?** (אחי, אתה לא חושב שהגיע זמן להרדים את הכלב?) "Brother, don't you think it's time you put the dog to sleep?"

Words of endearment, sincere and otherwise

Familiarity usually breeds contempt. In Israel, however, familiarity—or at least informality—also breeds words of endearment that are commonly used to address even complete strangers.

Masculine, Feminine

chamudi (חמודי), **chamuda** (חמודה): cute, cutie

matoki (מתוקי), **metuka** (מתוקה): sweetie

yakiri (יקירי), **yakirati** (יקירתי): my dear, darling

More intimate are a few meaningless words that just sound sweet. They can be used for anything dear to your heart: friends, lovers, children, fauna, flora.

kush-kush (קושקוש)

mush-mush (מושמוש)

tshush-kush (צ'ושקוש)

For addressing loved ones, these words are used:

eynyim sheli (עיניים שלי): my eyes

neshama (נשמה): soul

neshama sheli (נשמה שלי): my soul

chayim sheli (חיים שלי): my life

And then there are words that only lovers exchange. Don't use them on strangers! You might be misunderstood and lead someone on.

ahuvi (אהובי): my love (masculine)

ahuvati (אהובתי): my love (feminine)

yonati (יונתי): my dove

pashosh (פשוש): warbler, as in a small bird

You can create your own words of endearment by simply adding the syllable **le** (לה) at the end of a word to make it diminutive. If, say, you feel like being affectionate toward your friend Richard, call him Richard**le.** Your friend Suzy becomes Suzy**le.**

You can even attach **le** to a lover's term of endearment to make it not only more endearing but more personal. For instance, if you attach it to the word of the moment, **neshama** (soul), you get **neshamale,** which is far more affectionate than just **neshama.**

Words of endearment are sometimes used passive-aggressively.

Pay attention to the tone. If a sentence starts out with **matoki** (sweetie) said severely, prepare yourself for a blow. You might hear **Matoki, ani lo rotsa lirot otcha af pa-am yoter bachayim sheli** (מתוקי, אני לא רוצה לראות אותך אף פעם יותר בחיים שלי"): "Sweetie, I don't want to ever see you again in my life."

This practice is called **lehavi ota behafucha** (להביא אותה בהפוכה), "to bring it reversed." But that's not all. You can always turn the tables back and say **Yonati, lo hitkavanti lirot otach shenit** (יונתי, לא התכוונתי לראות אותך שנית): "My dove, I wasn't *planning* on seeing you again. This practice is called **hafuch al hafuch** (הפוך על הפוך), "reversed on reversed." You'll hear these two expressions and see them put into practice a lot in Israel.

Getting rid of people

If someone's presence is too much for you to bear, you can simply say **yala bye** (יללה ביי) and walk away.

> **yala** (יאללה): a word used for urging, as in
>
> **Yala, bo nelech!** (יללה בוא נלך!): Yala, let's go!

Yala can also be used as an answer:

> **Person 1:** Ba lecha lirot seret? (בא לך לראות סרט?)
> **Person 2:** Yala. (יללה.)
>
> **Person 1:** Do you want to go see a movie?
> **Person 2:** Let's go.

Bye (ביי) is borrowed from the English "bye-bye" and is often used as a greeting. **Yala bye** is not considered impolite; it

essentially means "I just remembered I have something important to do and have to leave abruptly." Israel is a hustling, bustling
place; saying **yala bye** and running along is common practice.

If you want the other person to leave, you can start by using
humor:

> **Lech tire im ani babayit** (לך תראה אם אני בבית): Go see if
> I'm home.

> **Chapes oti basivuv** (חפש אותי בסיבוב): Go look for me at the
> corner.

If the person you're trying to get rid off doesn't understand
humor and you have to use some heavier artillery, you can move to:

> **Uf li mehapanim!** (עוף לי מהפנים!): Fly away from my face!

If you need to escalate, try:

> **Tizdayen li mehapanim!** (תזדיין לי מהפנים!): Fuck off away
> from my face!

If he persists in bothering you and the only choice is to go
ballistic, there's always:

> **Lech chapes mi yenanea otcha!** (לך חפש מי ינענע אותך!): Go
> look for somebody to fuck (literally, "shake") you!

And if this doesn't work, turn to the next chapter, where I'll
teach you some real Hebrew swearing.

CHAPTER FOUR

Swearing and Insults

Israelis are the descendents of ultraorthodox Jews who for centuries sharpened their minds on the Holy Scriptures; a few decades of secularity haven't dulled us. Don't be fooled by the raging promiscuity in Tel Aviv. There's still no Hebrew word for "motherfucker." That's incest, for heaven's sake!

Profanity and vulgarity don't quite cut it here unless there's a dimension of wit or zaniness. If you want to make the natives laugh and pay attention, instead of just embarrassing yourself, you need to embellish your swearing. Get creative!

Okay:

Ima shelcha zona (אימא שלך זונה): Your mother is a whore.

Better:

Kama ima shelcha lokachat lemetsitsa?
(כמה אימא שלך לוקחת למציצה?): How much does your mother charge for a blow job?

The evolving curse

In 1948, when Israel was founded, there were practically no Hebrew curses. The language was dormant for nearly two thousand years—meaning we had only unsatisfactory biblical epithets, such as "May your right arm be forgotten" or "May your name be wiped out."

Luckily, immigrants from all parts of the world brought along their respective ways of swearing. We now have a solid, ever-evolving body of swearwords based on many languages and enabling us to deliver four-dimensional curses, such as this one, currently popular with the kids: **Halvay shetzayen gufa shel sus met bayarkon im hazayin hamchukmak shelcha** (הלוואי שתזיין גופה של סוס מת בירקון עם הזין המצ'וקמק שלך): "May you fuck the corpse of a dead horse in the Yarkon (river) with your shriveled dick."

Popular, but for how long? Like other curses emanating from the Internet, this one is probably destined to wear thin and morph into something else. Real Hebrew curses are short, on the mark, and ever evolving.

At some point, for instance, we got tired of repeatedly using the same old **kus emak** (כוס אמק), "your mother's cunt," from the Arabic. It lost ground to **kus ochtak** (כוס אוחתק), "your sister's pussy." After a while, we got tired of insulting sis and went back to mom. Meanwhile, **kus ochtak** grew into **hakus shel achotcha hatsola-at** (חכוס של אחותך הצולעת), "your limping sister's pussy," which eventually got shortened to **achotcha hatsola-at** (אחותך הצולעת), "your limping sister."

You can fire back with this all-purpose phrase whenever you're annoyed by stupid or accusing questions or comments.

For instance, to his wife's question, "Where were you so late?" (**Efo hayita kol kach meuchar?** איפה היית כל כך מאוחר?), a husband might reply, "At your limping sister's" (**Etzel achotcha hatsola-at** אצל אחותך הצולעת).

Or if someone were to say, "Look at you, you've gained so much weight." (**Tistakel al atsmecha, he-eleta kol kach harbe mishkal** תסתכל על עצמך, העלית כל כך הרבה משקל), the correct response might be, "Your limping sister gained weight" (**Acotcha hatsola-at alta bamishkal** אחותך הצולעת עלתה במשקל).

The other amen

"Amen" is usually said at the end of a prayer. In real Hebrew cursing, it is said at the beginning of the imprecation.

> **Amen, she-elokim yohav otcha veyikach otcha kvar elav**
> (אמן, שאלוקים יאהב אותך וייקח אותך כבר אליו): Amen, may God love you and immediately take you to Him.

> **Amen, shetsiporey gan eden kvar yehenu mimcha**
> (אמן, שציפורי גן-עדן כבר ייהנו ממך): Amen, may the birds of paradise soon enjoy you.

> **Amen, shekelev rechov jinji iver ya-anos et ima shelcha vegam et achotcha**
> (אמן, שכלב רחוב ג'ינג'י עיוור יאנוס את האימא שלך וגם את אחותך): Amen, may a blind, red, stray dog rape your mother, and your sister, too.

Animal insults

Israelis love animals, from fish and hamsters to snakes and turtles, and, of course, cats and dogs. Walk around Tel Aviv and you'll feel like you're in an open zoo for stray cats. In almost

every building you'll find a cat-loving person who feeds these strays. Once in a while the felines are rounded up and neutered. Cats rule the city; they lie in the sun oblivious to the many dogs (usually pets) roaming around. Animal rights are aggressively pursued by a strong organization called **Tnu Lachayot Lichyot** (תנו לחיות לחיות): Let Animals Live.

Personally, I like my animals well done, on a plate, and preferably kosher, but most Israelis like them best in their slang.

chaidak (חיידק): germ, an insignificant person who causes trouble

pishpesh (פשפש): flea, a physically or mentally small person; someone who doesn't leave you alone

juk (ג'וק): cockroach, a despicable person or small gadget

tola-at (תולעת): worm, a spineless person

kuter (קוטר): tomcat, a person who nags and nags; from Yiddish and applicable to both sexes

kof (קוף): monkey, an ugly person

chazir (חזיר): pig, a dirty, fat, sleazy person

chamor (חמור): donkey, a stupid person

para (פרה): cow, a stupid person

behema (בהמה): beast, a rude, vulgar, stupid, sleazy, uneducated person

When you get on the Almighty's nerves

I already mentioned that biblical curses don't always meet the demands of our modern stresses. But I don't want to leave you with the impression that they haven't enriched the contemporary Israeli vocabulary.

In the Sinai desert, when the Israelites complained to Moses that they'd had enough of manna and wanted real food—meat, fish, or vegetables—G-D told Moses he would give them meat **ad asher yetse meapchem** (עד אשר יצא מאפכם), "until it comes out of your nostrils" (Numbers 11:20). This phrase is still very much in use when Israelis are fed up with something.

For example, **Nimas li kvar lichtov et hasefer haze, hu yotse li meha-af** (נמאס לי כבר לכתוב את הספר הזה, הוא יוצא לי מהאף): "I'm fed up, already, with writing this book; it's coming out of my nostrils."

You can also say, to the same effect, **Yotse li mehatachat** (יוצא לי מהתחת): "It's coming out of my ass."

Or better yet, **Yotse li mekol hachorim** (יוצא לי מכל החורים): "It's coming out of all my holes."

But for my money, G-D's word still rules.

CHAPTER FIVE

Bodily Functions and Body Parts

The real Hebrew ass and things associated with it

When an Israeli says a person or a situation is **chara** (חרא), "shit," he is dead serious. He means that this is the bottom line where all fun stops and the situation turns decidedly bad. Pessimistic Israelis compare life to hair growing in the ass: short, black, and shitty.

Akuz (עכוז) is the polite word for "buttocks." In the street, it's usually used with the word **soed** (סועד), "he/she dines," as part of an elegant, funny expression that describes someone enjoying anal sex: **soed ba-akuz** (סועד בעכוז), "dines in the buttocks."

Yashvan (ישבן), "sitter," is a cute way of saying "ass" without any negative connotations. It's usually used when describing a nice, curvy, female ass. If you'd like to turn that into a swear, add **menashek** (מנשק), "kisser." You'll get **menashek yashvanim** (מנשק ישבנים), which means "ass-kisser."

Achorayim (אחוריים) is equivalent to "behind" and is seldom used.

Tusik (טוסיק) comes from the Yiddish word for "butt," *toches*. This innocent word is mainly used when talking about a baby's bottom. But when you add **ochel** (אוכל), "eats," you get **ochel batusik** (בטוסיק), which is a sweet way to say "gay" and literally translates to "eats in that scrumptiously cute little behind of his."

The most common swearword for "ass" is **tachat** (תחת), which literally means "under."

Here are some examples of its use:

Shak li batachat (שק לי בתחת): Kiss my ass.

Kanes li latachat (כנס לי לתחת): Literally, "Get into my ass." This is by no means an invitation to anal sex but rather something along the lines of "get back to where you belong, you piece of shit." To make it more colorful say:

> **Kanes li latachat vetse metsupe** (כנס לי לתחת וצא מצופה): Get into my ass and come out coated.

lakekan tachat (לקקן תחת): ass-licker

likroa et hatachat (לקרוע את התחת): a strenuous endeavor; literally, "ripped the ass"

meanyen et hatachat sheli (מעניין את התחת שלי): tell it to my ass; literally, "it interests my ass"

partsuf tachat (פרצוף תחת): ass face

kisuy tachat (כיסוי תחת): ass covering; that is, a sound alibi for any possible wrongdoing

litfos tachat (לתפוש תחת): to catch an ass, meaning to get comfortable in a situation and feel secure enough to take command

sipur mehatachat (סיפור מהתחת): a story from the ass; that is, an unpleasant, tiresome affair that requires a lot of hustle to resolve; for example, when you lose your passport, money, and all your credit cards in a foreign land

tachat male chara (תחת מלא חרא): an ugly female's ass; literally, "an ass filled with shit"

niftach lo hatachat (נפתח לו התחת): went to his head; literally, "his ass got opened"

mizdayen batachat (מזדיין בתחת): a person who fucks in the ass (equivalent to "faggot")

Totsi et haetsba mehatachat (תוציא את האצבע מהתחת): Take your finger out of your ass.

Shit, from the clinical to the crude

tsoa (צואה): excrement

kaki (קקי): poop
    Ima, yesh li kaki (אמא יש לי קקי): Mommy, I have to poop.

kaka (קקה): shit; used to describe a person, a thing, or situation that is shitty

drek (דרעק): a really shitty person; from Yiddish

chara (חרא): Real shit. The most common word in street talk and swearing, it means the final, useless, and smelly stage of the digestive process. When applied, for instance, to a car, it means it's the worst lemon you could imagine.

chatichat chara (חתיכת חרא): Piece of shit. A terminally motherfucking bastard you'd better erase immediately from your contact list.

achal chara (אכל חרא): to put up with a lot of shit; literally, "ate shit"

lecharben (לחרבן): to shit; also, to ruin

> **Hahorim shela bau baemtsa vechirbnu lanu et kol hazi-yun** (ההורים שלה באו באמצע וחרבנו לנו את כל הזיון): Her parents walked in on us and ruined our screwing.

lehitcharben (להתחרבן): to get shit on; can mean (a) to get screwed (not sexually) or (b) to get one's period

Farting etiquette

Haifa is built on the slopes of Mount Carmel. When a new house is being built, they have to blow up the hillside with dynamite. The head blaster always shouts out **Varda, varda!** (ורדה!), from the Arabic for "explosion." So before one farts, it's polite to shout the same warning. Afterward it's good manners to say **chatnaga** (חתנגה), taking full responsibility for the ensuing stench. I used to say it a lot just to watch my friends running frantically for cover.

When you want to say "bullshit!"

Real Hebrew doesn't have an exact translation for "bullshit," but there are a few good ways to express more or less the same idea.

bilbul beytsim (בלבול ביצים): confusing to the balls (testicles)

bilbul moach (בלבול מוח): confusing to the brain

zibuley sechel (זיבולי שכל): mind trashing

ziyun moach (זיון מוח): brain fucking; closest to the true meaning of the English "bullshit" and the expression most often used

The real Hebrew penis

There is a very clever observation in the Talmud: "A man has a small limb; if he starves it, it's sated; if he sates it, it is hungry" (**Ever katan yesh lo la-adam, marivo savea, masbio raev**

44   *Danny Ben Israel*

(אבר קטן יש לו לאדם, מרעיבו שבע, משביעו רעב). No need for explanation, don't you think?

There are many kinds of dicks in Hebrew and many words to describe them.

Young boys beginning wonderful friendships with their weenies are in the habit of nicknaming them. The most common nickname in real Hebrew is **Yochanan** (יוחנן), a nerdy Israeli name equivalent to John and a humorous way to refer affectionately to one's own dick.

> **bulbul** (בולבול): A baby's dick. When used for a grown-up, it may be considered an insulting comment about the size of his dick.
>
> **pots** (פוץ): Yiddish word for a dick, used mainly to describe a really stupid motherfucker.
>
> **shmok** (שמוק): Prick (also Yiddish). As in "a real prick." The diminutive form, **shmekkl** (שמקל), means an itty-bitty penis.
>
> **shtrungul** (שטרונגול): A nicely developed hard dick. The verb form, **leshtrangel** (לשטרנגל), means to fuck someone to the bone, not necessarily sexually.

Zayin (זין), the most common word for a dick, also means "weapon" and is widely used to say "definitely not" (though it's not as strong as **zubi**). **Zayin** started as a polite way to say "penis" in Yiddish. In Yiddish a dick is commonly called a *shvants* (tail), like *Schwanz* in German. In Hebrew the word becomes **zanav** (זנב), and to avoid any profanity Jews would only say the word's first letter, **zayin** (the seventh letter in the Hebrew alphabet). When Yiddish-speaking Jews immigrated to Israel, the name of that letter lost all its innocence and took on the meaning it has today.

Other forms of **zayin**:

lezayen (לזיין): to fuck; literally, "to dick"

lech tizdayen (לך תזדיין): go fuck yourself; literally, "go dick yourself"

al hazayin (על הזין): fuck it; literally, "on the dick"

Lo sam zayin (לא שם זין): I don't give a fuck. Literally, "I don't give a dick."

zayin ba-ayin (זין בעין): fuck you; literally, "a prick in your eye"

Penis size

Some terminology to help a guy boast (given in order from smallest to biggest):

meuvzar (מאובזר): accessorized; doesn't reveal the actual size but means the proprietor doesn't think it's too small

metsuyad heytev (מצויד היטב): well hung

kli marshim (כלי מרשים): impressive tool

kli kli (כלי כלי): a tool tool (repeating the word leaves no doubt—it's definitely big!)

zayin gadol (זין גדול): big dick

eyvar anak (איבר ענק): giant organ

These terms are mostly used in online sex ads.

kli kli

The real Hebrew vagina

Pot (פות) is the polite word for a vagina. Some other popular terms are:

> **manoah** (מנוע): a sizzling hot pussy; literally, "engine"
>
> **manush** (מנוש): a tender pussy
>
> **kus** (כוס): cunt (the most common word used for a vagina)

More sexual anatomy

shadayim (שדיים): breast

pitmot (פטמות): nipples

dagdegan (דגדגן): clitoris

beytsim (ביצים): balls

lashon (לשון): tongue

Common phrases and idioms that incorporate body parts

kaved lavan (כבד לבן): a person who is always calm; literally, "white liver"

musar klayot (מוסר כליות): guilty conscience; literally, "moral kidney"

kshe oref (קשה עורף): stubborn; literally, "hard nape," as in "stiff necked"

charon af (חרון אף): anger; literally, "nose wrath"

im ha-af lemata (עם האף למטה): depressed, unsatisfied; literally, "down in the nose"

neshama beapo (נשמה באפו): alive; literally, "soul in the nose"

akev betsad agudal (עקב בצד אגודל): walking very carefully; literally, "with your heel at the side of the thumb"

shfal lev (שפל לב): humble; literally, "low hearted"

Likpots meal lapupik.

lisod et halev (לסעוד את הלב): to eat; literally, "to feed the heart"

ayin tsara (עין צרה): envious; literally, "narrow eyed"

likpots meal lapupik (לקפוץ מעל לפופיק): to get excited; literally, "to jump above your belly button"

nafal libo bekirbo (נפל ליבו בקרבו): to be scared shitless; literally, "to have your heart fall"

pik birkayim (פיק ברכיים): shaky knees, as in feeling fear; literally, "knee wobble"

CHAPTER SIX

Sex

Straight sex

Consensual heterosexual sex is not considered a sin in Judaism. On the contrary, God commanded Adam and Eve to "be fruitful and multiply and replenish the earth" (**pru urevu umalu et ha-aretz** פרו ורבו ומלאו את הארץ).

Israelis are friendly people. When someone is friendly toward you, it doesn't necessarily mean they are sexually interested. If they are they'll be direct about it, especially the women, who are independent and strong-minded. Don't play games: they'll see right through you.

A word of warning: as a country Israel is very sensitive to sexual harassment, molestation, or coercion; an unconfirmed suspicion may land you in jail. A recent Israeli president, Moshe Katsav, had to resign and face trial for allegedly forcing himself on his secretary.

Let's start with the traditional and move to the less conventional.

The kosher fuck

First of all, the ultra religious married couple can get it on only during two weeks out of four. Touching is off-limits for one week during **veset** (וסת), or menstruation (literally, "control," and also known as **machzor** מחזור, "cycle," or **degel adom** דגל אדום, "red flag"). The week after that the wife has to purify herself and sex continues to be forbidden. The couple can only have sex when the woman is in full bloom; i.e., during **biyuts** (ביוץ), "ovulation." And only if she wants to. The man can't just jump her at any time. He has to wait patiently until they're in bed in pitch dark-ness. Then he throws his yarmulke to her side of the bed. If she's not in the mood, she doesn't have to fake a headache; she just throws the yarmulke back. There's nothing he can do but take a cold shower; divine law forbids **leonen** (לאונן), "masturbation."

If she keeps the yarmulke, he has to put a sheet between his body and hers, with a hole in the middle to allow genital access. Penetration at last! Then he's commanded to screw "as if forced by the demon" (**kemi shekfao hashed** כמי שכפאו השד). That's what the Talmud says, and the Talmud is law!

Orthodox Jews refer to having sex as **mitsvat pru urevu** (מצוות פרו ורבו), "the commandment to be fruitful and multiply." Or they might use the more subtle euphemism **mikchol besh-foferet** (מכחול בשפופרת), "a paintbrush in a paint tube." Here is some other sexual terminology the Orthodox use:

oneg shabat (עונג שבת): Sabbath pleasures

biah (ביאה): coming

mashkin shalom (משכין שלום): penis; literally, "one who brings peace"

hamakom (המקום): vagina; literally, "the place"

litpos ziyun

To an Orthodox Jew, sex is strictly for reproduction; for amusement he dwells on the Holy Scriptures.

Finding a partner and getting it on secular-style

Due to the mixing of many ethnic groups, we have a lot of pretty boys and girls in Israel. Before you go out hunting, here are a few useful words:

chaticha (חתיכה): an attractive woman; literally, "piece"

chatich (חתיך): an attractive man

kusit (כוסית): a sexy girl

kuson (כוסון): a sexy guy

   both derived from **kus** (cunt)

akuma (עקומה): unattractive woman; literally, "crooked"

akum (עקום): unattractive man; literally, "crooked"

shafa (שפה): beautiful young girl

yafyuf (יפיוף): handsome young boy

lehatchil (להתחיל): to woo; literally, "to start"

hemyat meayim (המיית מעיים): longing; literally, "murmuring intestines"

neshika (נשיקה): a kiss

lishloach yadayim (לשלוח ידיים): to touch someone in a sexual way; literally, "to send hands"

kocho bemotnav (כוחו במותניו): virile; literally, "his power is in his loin"

parpar (פרפר): one who fucks around; literally, "butterfly" (from their habit of flying from flower to flower)

lehitparper (להתפרפר): to fuck around

litpos ziyun (לתפוס זיון): To have sex. This is the most common way to say this. Literally, "to catch a fuck."

chafuz (חפוז): a quickie

ligmor (לגמור): to come; literally, "to finish"

charman (חרמן): horny (masculine)

charmanit (חרמנית): horny (feminine)

lehitcharmen (להתחרמן): to get horny

lehitchashesh (להתחשש): necking

lehitmazmez (להתמזמז): making out

stuts (סטוץ): one-night stand

notenet (נותנת): a girl who's easy, who gives out

seret kachol (סרט כחול): porno; literally, "blue movie"

Yesh mazav? (יש מצב?): Is there a possibility I could have sex with you?

Etsly o etslech? (אצלי או אצלך?): My place or yours?

titpashet (תתפשט): get undressed (masculine)

titpashti (תתפשטי): get undressed (feminine)

beadinut (בעדינות): gently

toridi et hachaziya (תורידי את החזייה): take off your bra

al hamita (על המיטה): on the bed

beamidah (בעמידה): standing

leat (לאט): slowly

timtsots li et hapitma (תמצוץ לי את הפטמה): suck my nipple

latfi li oto (לטפי לי אותו): stroke it

terdi li (תרדי לי): go down on me

bli shinayim (בלי שיניים): no teeth

tochal oti (תאכל אותי): eat me

tachnis li (תכניס לי): put it in me

yoter amok (יותר עמוק): deeper

chazak yoter (חזק יותר): harder

maher yoter (מהר יותר): faster

tistovevi (תסתובבי): turn around

lo batachat (לא בתחת): not in the ass

tenasi (תנסי): try it

koev (כואב): it hurts

tiftechi (תפתחי): open up

totsi miyad (וציא מיד): take it out immediately

lo bekoach (לא בכוח): not with force

al habirkayim (על הברכיים): on your knees

ad hasof (עד הסוף): all the way; literally, "to the end"

shvi alay (שבי עלי): sit on me

sachki leatsmech (שחקי לעצמך): play with yourself

al tigmor chake li (אל תגמור חכה לי): don't come, wait for me

al tafsik (אל תפסיק): don't stop

achshav (עכשיו): now

ani gomeret (אני גומרת): I'm coming

Haya lecha tov? (?היה לך טוב): Was it good for you?

Likro lach monit? (?לקרא לך מונית): Shall I call you a cab?

If by chance you don't score, there are two things you can do. You can **lehavi ota bayad** (להביא אותה ביד), "bring it with the hand" (or as mentioned in chapter 1: **la-asot bayad**, "to do in the hand"), or you can go to a massage parlor and for about fifty dollars (two hundred shekels) get the whole treatment. Israel has many such places, stocked with pretty Eastern European girls. A lot of single Israeli men prefer visiting the friendly neighborhood massage parlor to spending twice as much on a date, which doesn't always lead to sex. Many Israeli husbands visit their favorite working girl once a week or so and go home relaxed, so they can be nice to their wife, patient with the kids, and have no desire to kick the dog. Working girls save a lot of marriages.

There are two ways to refer to a woman who has a lot of sex. A **zona** (זונה) is one who does it for money (a prostitute), and a **sharmuta** (שרמוטה) does it for her own pleasure.

There arose a need for a more liberal-toned word, and up one popped. The politically correct term for a girl who sleeps around is **sharlila** (שרלילה). Doesn't it sound nicer? It simply means a girl who enjoys having sex with no shame or guilt attached to it.

If you're a woman visiting Israel and need to get your kicks, check out the local gigolos. Israel has its fair share, and they prefer foreign girls. They're well dressed and groomed, and will hit on you in all the tourist spots. There is no reason for a woman to stay lonely in Israel if she's willing to adjust her standards.

Real Hebrew idioms for having sex

lidfok (לדפוק): to knock

livdok shemen (לבדוק שמן): to check the oil

leharim (להרים): to lift

leakem (לעקם): to bend

lehashchil (להשחיל): to thread

lidchof (לדחוף): to shove

litchon (לטחון): to grind

la-akots (לעקוץ): to sting

litkoa (לתקוע): to thrust

LGBT: lesbian, gay, bisexual, and transgender

The most common term for homosexuals these days is **ge-eh** (גאה): literally, "proud." If you're bisexual, you're **du** (דו), "bi." In Israel you can openly show your affection for your partner. You're especially safe in Tel Aviv, one of the gay capitals of the world, with magnificent love parades and well-organized and vociferous gay and lesbian organizations.

Israel, like the rest of the world, is under the spell of the largest global religion ever: political correctness. A guy I know very well went with his lover to a supermarket late one night and intentionally provoked the cashier by conspicuously necking and being obnoxious. The cashier wasn't thrilled and gave them a piece of his mind. Two days later the guy filed a complaint and got handsomely and apologetically compensated, while the poor cashier—whom I assume hardly made ends meet, working the graveyard shift for peanuts—got fired. People in authority always sway with the prevailing winds.

For many years the only slang word for "gay" was **nablus** (נבלוס), like the ancient West Bank city of the same name. The Bible refers to Abraham passing through Nablus on his way to the Promised Land and offering his first sacrifice to his newly found G-D. The city was destroyed in the ninth century BC by the Assyrians, then revived by the Hellenes (who erected a famous temple to Zeus) and taken over in turn by the Romans, the Byzantines, the Arabs, and (after World War I) the Brits. In the Arab world, Nablus is a synonym for homosexuality. I'm not sure which of the many conquerors made homosexuality big there.

Nablus is also used as a verb:

lenables (לנבלס): to fuck in the ass

lehitnables (להתנבלס): to get fucked in the ass

A canonical gay lexicon, *Even-Shoshan,* was published in the 1990s. The title is a dig at Abraham Even-Shoshan, editor of the authoritative dictionary of modern Hebrew.

Here are some terms from *Even-Shoshan* that are still current.

uchtcha (אוחצ'ה): Sis. Gay people use this to refer to themselves and each other. It is short for **achot sheli** (אחות שלי), "my sister." The plural is **uchtchot** (אוחצ'ות).

jong (ג'ונג): penis

jordel (ג'ורדל): From the French *bordel* (brothel) and *jardin* (garden). Refers to the magnificent **Gan Ha'atzmaut** (גן העצמאות), or Independence Garden, a Tel Aviv park on a cliff overlooking the sea. Here gay men cruise, day and night, looking for casual sex (**min mizdamen** מין מזדמן), which is usually performed on-site. Although it has lost some of its glory to the Internet, the park is still frequented by those who like anonymity. It is also known as **hasifriya** (הספרייה), "the library."

danah (דנה): A synonym for the first name of singer Dana International, the quintessential Israeli transsexual diva, a goddess who brought a lot of pride to Israel, especially its gay community, when her song "Diva" won first place in the 1998 Eurovision Song Contest.

histeri (היסטרי): very impressive, extraordinary; literally, "hysterical"

viadja (ויאג'ה): an old homosexual; from the Spanish *vieja*, "old woman"

vison (ויזון): a cunt; from the French *vison*, "mink"

jermij (ז'רמיז): stunning

chilul (חילול): giving a blow job; literally, "blowing the flute," from **chalil** (חליל), "flute"

kus original (כוס אוריגינל): female by birth; literally, "original cunt"

kus flash (כוס פלאש): flattening of the penis for a more feminine appearance; literally, "instant cunt"

lehapil (להפיל): to trick a straight person into having sex with a homosexual; literally, "to trip someone"

lird (לירד): a handsome dude; from "lord"

manfuach (מנפוח): a muscular guy; from **nafuach** (נפוח), "blown up"

ma-ayana (מעיינה): a stupid, foolish girl; a word in the Iraqi Arabic vernacular

flega (פלגה): a stupid girl; from "phlegmatic"

markita (מרקיטה): extremely feminine gay male; from the Italian *mercato*, "market"

overet (עוברת): a woman who successfully passes as a man; literally, "passes"

kukitsa (קוקיצה): effeminate homosexual

Hu mitpalel beveyt hakneset shelanu?
(הוא מתפלל בבית הכנסת שלנו?): Literally, "Does he pray in our synagogue?" In other words, "Is he gay?"

toridi et ha-ananas (תורידי את האננס): stop being so stiff, relax; literally, "take off the pineapple"

tatkini ma-alit (תתקיני מעלית): get with it, start living in the twenty-first century; literally, "install an elevator"

lalechet al hashtrich (ללכת על השטריך): To go out looking for sex. From the German *gehen am Strich*, "walking the line." Refers to a bygone time when prostitutes were forbidden to cross a line drawn down the sidewalk.

Being gay in Tel Aviv is an advantage, but outside the big city use discretion. These are some pejoratives you might hear:

menashneshet meshulashim (מנשנשת משולשים): lesbian; literally, "munches triangle"

homo (הומו)

mitromem (מתרומם): lifter

noshech kariot (נושך כריות): pillow biter

bochesh bashoko (בוחש בשוקו): stirring the chocolate

maflits kotage (מפליץ קוטאגי): farts cottage cheese

meachzev horim (מאכזב הורים): parents' disappointment

mitkofef (מתכופף): one who bends over

mithapech (מתהפך): one who turns over

noten batachat (נותן בתחת): gives it in the ass

mekabel batachat (מקבל בתחת): takes it in the ass

tochen (טוחן): one who fucks; literally, "mills"

nitchan (נטחן): the one who is getting fucked; literally, "getting milled"

Transgender: A Story

Koksinel (קוקסינל), "transgender," comes from the French word *coccinelle*, which means "ladybug." In the mid-1960s, when Israelis didn't know what transgender was, a musical act from Paris, Coccinelle, came to perform. She left such an impression on this young, provincial country that we adopted her name.

I had the pleasure of intimately encountering Coccinelle and her group. I was starring in a hit musical, but I couldn't refuse a generous offer to join a cabaret show near the theater. Just before

midnight, I would hurry over to the club, still wearing makeup and nervous about hitting the high C in my grand finale. Coccinelle followed my act.

During the first week, no one suspected that the members of this girl group were all born male—the club management kept the secret. A lot of innocent men tried to make out with the girls, including me. I went for the star, the prettiest, most-sophisticated lady I'd ever seen. We took long walks on the beach, held hands, and kissed gently under the moonlight. I wanted to have her, of course, but each time my hands started wandering, she said in her velvety alto, "Ce n'est pas une bonne idée, mon chou" ("It's not a good idea, sweetie"). Our romance lasted a whole week, until one night after the show, as I was relieving myself at the urinal, who do you think came in? *Mon amour, ma bien-aimée*— my beloved! Without paying attention to me, she casually took out a huge, uncircumcised penis (**zayin arel gadol** זין ערל גדול) and started urinating right next to me.

I was dumbfounded. This was a little too much for a country boy to grasp. I knew uncircumcised dicks existed and was able to deduce that the sheath covering the chiseled tip must be the foreskin. But a woman with a dick was something I'd never considered.

I had noticed her pronounced Adam's apple, big limbs, and low voice, but without making the connection. While I was trying to figure out how the hell to react, the door opened and everybody marched in—the musicians, waiters, managers, and the rest of the transvestites—all pointing at me and laughing.

What hurt most wasn't finding out that the woman I'd been tenderly kissing was a man, or being exposed as a yokel (our picture even appeared in a tabloid). It was her mischievous and amused look as everyone laughed at me in the bathroom. She'd set me up. I never spoke to her again, even when I noticed she was crying. After the last show, she came up to me, saying she wanted to explain. I just said, "Trop tard, mon amour" ("Too late, my love"), and left dramatically, without looking back. I was still very young.

Ever since then there have been rumors about my sexuality. It would be beneath me to deny them. Besides, they never hurt my sex life. For many women, having sex with a gay guy is something to brag about, like a cherished trophy.

Swapping and swinging

A friend of mine says swinging Israeli-style is too bourgeois for his taste. Typically, at the end of the night, when no one has any juice left, the participants gather in the living room, naked or half-naked, and make small talk—the women about the best schools and shops, the men about politics and sports.

Here is some swinger vocabulary:

chilufey zugot (חילופי זוגות): couple swapping

hachlafot (החלפות): swapping

zigzugim (זיגזוגים): swapping; from **zug** (זוג), "couple," and the English "zigzag"

There are many ways to say "orgy." You can simply use the English word, **orgy** (אורגיה), or choose any of these options:

shchav-rav (שכב-רב): multi-lay

mesibat cheshek (מסיבת חשק): desire party

al achat kama vechama (על אחת כמה וכמה): gang bang; literally, "a few and a few on one"

mesiba rabat mishtatfim (מסיבה רבת משתתפים): multipar-
ticipant party

pinukei mita (פינוקי מיטה): bed pampering

hitarbevut (התערבבות): mixing

S-M and BDSM

Sadomasochism, or S-M, is known in Hebrew as **sado-mazo**
(סאדו-מאזו). The acronym **BDSM** (בדס'מ) is pronounced as in
English and comprises **kshirot** (קשירות), "bondage"; **tsiyut** (ציות),
"discipline"; **sadistiut** (סדיסטיות), "sadism"; and—again the same
as in English—**masochism** (מסוכיזם).

Israel, in tune with the rest of the Western world, has opened
every closet and anything goes. The BDSM club **Donjon** (דנג'ן), or
the Dungeon, opened in 2002 in Jaffa. Crowds flocked there but
mainly to watch—only a few participated. When the club's neigh-
bors went to court to have the place shut, hundreds of aficionados
proudly demonstrated in front of the courthouse. Since then
BDSM has been recognized here as an alternative lifestyle.

Two BDSM communities, Domdomina and the Cage, have
Web sites. Applicants are closely screened and rules are strictly
enforced, all with a matter-of-fact Israeli attitude. If you suspect
that this is your cup of tea, here is your chance to check it out in
a **sviva betucha** (סביבה בטוחה), "safe environment."

From the Latin word *domina*, meaning "mistress" or "lady,"
come the two Hebrew words for a dominatrix: **domit** (דומית) and
domina (דומינה). Here are some other ways to address her:

malka (מלכה): queen

gvira (גבירה): lady

elila (אלילה): goddess

A master, **adon** (אדון), is also known as:

dom (דום): dom

sholet (שולט): ruler

elyon (עליון): upper

The words for "sexual slave" are gender specific: **eved** (עבד), masculine, and **shifcha** (שפחה), feminine. A handful of other terms also vary with gender.

Masculine, Feminine

nishlat (נשלט), **nishletet** (נשלטת): dominated

kanua (כנוע), **knuaa** (כנועה): submissive

tachton (תחתון): lower (no feminine)

sab (סאב), **sabit** (סאבית): submissive

Eved min (עבד מין) is the slave of a dominatrix, not necessarily for sex, but mostly for doing her chores.

Masters often address slaves of both genders with these words:

kelev (כלב): dog

zona (זונה): whore

efes (אפס): zero

Someone who is not really into BDSM and comes only to watch is **vanil** (וניל), "vinyl." In Hebrew, **vanil** is pronounced like "vanilla," and especially so in the plural, **vanila** (ונילה).

Since BDSM is practiced among consenting adults, partners agree on a word that halts the action if it gets too rough.

This is known as a **milat bitachon** (מילת ביטחון), "safety word."
Mischakey katse (משחקי קצה) is "edge play," which is when the
partners agree on practicing BDSM without limits and with no
safety word.

    Mischakey tafkidim (משחקי תפקידים) means "role-playing."
A person capable of switching roles from slave to master, and
vice versa, is a "switcher": **mitchalef** (מתחלף) for a man and
mitchalefet (מתחלפת) for a woman.

CHAPTER SEVEN

Drugs and Thugs

Alcohol

Russians make up the largest ethnic group in Israel. They started coming at the beginning of the twentieth century and kept on coming. When communism crumbled, they came by the millions, overwhelmed the country, and had quite an impact on the language and culture.

They also had an effect on Israeli drinking habits. Before the Russians came, there were no drinking habits. My own theory is that Israelis never really took to drinking because of the **yayin patishim** (יין פטישים), or "hammers wine," served by the army to sanctify the Sabbath at Friday dinner. Most of us drank it to get drunk, which is exactly what the top brass was trying to prevent by serving this unpalatable concoction (low in alcohol but loaded with sugar). We got wasted and the headaches we woke up to felt like hammers in our heads—hence the name. After three years of service, nobody wanted to touch the stuff. If you mention **yayin patishim** to Israelis of my generation, their eyes will light up, not because of the taste of the wine, but because of the reminder of younger days. These days you see drunkards with bottles of vodka, wobbling and cursing away on street corners, like in any normal country.

Young Israelis mainly drink vodka as a chaser to Red Bull. That's why a drink is actually called **chaser** (צ'יסר).

Drug vocabulary

Before we move to the illegal drugs, here are some words and phrases for the different states of mind they induce, starting with the default.

sachi (סחי): sober; from Arabic, meaning "tile"

balbala (בלבלה): bewilderment

sutul (סוטול): a high

mastul (מסטול): to be high

satlan (סטלן): a person who regularly gets high

lehistatel (להסתטל): to get high

dalka (דלקה): flash, or high from the first hit

shagat (שגעת): raving, or out of control

menat yeter (מנת-יתר): overdose

afifon (עפיפון): high as a kite

lehitchare (להתחרע): to overdo it, with no limits

shanty (שאנטי): Inner peace. From the Sanskrit word *shanti*. World-roaming Israeli backpackers brought this word back from India. It's used for the peaceful stage in being high, where life seems beautiful with no clouds on the horizon.

And where do people reach these states? Often at a **mesibat samim** (מסיבת סמים), "drug party."

Marijuana, or pot, has its own nomenclature for getting high:

litpos rosh (לתפוש ראש): to get high; literally, "to catch a head"

rosh tov (ראש טוב): A pleasant high. Literally, "a good head." It can also mean a person with a good head on his shoulders. **Rosh** (ראש), the word for "head," also makes a pot-themed appearance in the saying, **Afilu satlan gadol morid lifamim rosh katan** (אפילו סטלן גדול מוריד לפעמים ראש קטן): "Even a big pothead sometimes smokes a small head." This refers to smoking a mixture of pot and tobacco in a water pipe to the point that ashes fall into the water.

Pot

Pot is widely used in Israel, as in any other civilized country. It comes in two forms: marijuana, preferred by youngsters, and good old hashish, which comes from grass and is preferred by old-timers.

esev (עשב): Grass, marijuana. There isn't too much around and most of it is homegrown. In Israel it's usually smoked like hashish; i.e., mixed with tobacco.

yarok (ירוק): green

chashish (חשיש): hashish; from the Arabic for "grass"

Also known as:
kef (כֵּיף): fun
nafas (נפאס): spirit
chumi (חומי): brownie

chomer (חומר): stuff, a common name for all drugs

In one aspect Israel is fortunate to have Lebanon as its northern neighbor. For ages Lebanon manufactured the finest hashish in the world. It used to come in flat two-hundred-gram chunks wrapped in white cotton cloth sacks (**sakim** שקים) with the manufacturer's insignia stamped proudly on them. A sack was divided into sixteen pieces, each sold on the street as an **etsba** (אצבע), "a finger." Today hashish is still being sold on the street in "fingers," but they have become much smaller and poorer in quality.

For the last few years, the Lebanese border has been too carefully watched to permit smuggling. So don't expect high-quality hash in Israel. Like the rest of the Western world, especially Europe, Israel is flooded with cheap Moroccan stuff that's part hashish and part various enhancers such as sleeping pills and methadone. Smoking it can make you groggy and give you a headache.

Such pot is called **chashab** (חש"ב), an abbreviation of **chomer shelo ba barosh** (חומר שלא בא בראש), "stuff that doesn't get to the head." I'm proud to say that I was present when this slang word was born. I didn't think much of it until I started hearing it regularly on the streets. Lee Ish-Kassit, an aspiring young singer-songwriter and one of my many adopted nephews, said one night at a recording studio:

"I can't stand this **chashab** anymore. I'm moving to Amsterdam" (**Ani lo yachol yoter im hachashab haze, ani over leamsterdam** אני לא יכול יותר עם החש"ב הזה, אני עובר לאמסטרדם).

I told him that **chashab** was a stupid word, and he bet me it

Ani lo yachol yoter im hachashab
haze, ani over leamsterdam.

would catch on. I replied that he smoked too much. But in the end I was proven wrong.

Here are more words associated with pot:

buf (בוף): a small piece of hash, enough for a joint or two

ksesa (קססה): a mixture of tobacco and pot

farsh (פארש): plain tobacco

jontil (ז'ונטיל): a smooth joint

faisal (פייסל): a joint made of two cigarettes put together

tsingale (צינגלה): a regular joint

megulgelet (מגולגלת): a rolled joint

shachta (שכטה): a drag

bang (באנג): a water pipe

Heavier stuff

opyum (אופיום): opium

Also known as:
shachor (שחור): black
shwartse (שוורצה): black; from Yiddish

bizra (ביזרה): a small piece of opium

Opium gives one the ultimate high—total connection to one-self. But, as with most good things in life, the price is high:

krize (קריז): withdrawal symptoms

duda (דודה): cravings; from the Arabic for "worm"

It's difficult to score decent opium these days, since there is no demand. The traditional users, mainly Arabs and old Persian and Afghani Jews, are fading away, and the younger generation prefers powders. The little opium that trickles into the country is mainly **baladi** (בלאדי), "local," which is usually grown by bedouins in the Sinai desert. It's not very potent but is laced with sweet dates, which makes it easier to take.

One winter day in 1975, the opium dealers announced to their clients that there would be no more opium but only heroin, a drug previously unknown here. The drug scene changed completely. Instead of psychedelic flower children, we got junkies and criminals—much like what happened in San Francisco's Haight-Ashbury in the late sixties and early seventies.

In Israel heroin is mostly snorted, like cocaine, and has only a few Hebrew nicknames:

> **lavan** (לבן): white
>
> **drek** (דרעק): shit; from Yiddish

A cruder, cheaper form of heroin is **kok parsi** (קוק פרסי), "Persian coke." This powder isn't pure enough to sniff, so it's smoked by a process known in English as "chasing the dragon" and in Hebrew as **leharits** (להריץ), "making it run." This is similar to the way one takes crack cocaine: A small amount of the stuff is placed on a tinfoil sheet and a flame is held underneath to melt it and make it run. The user chases it with a tin straw in his mouth and inhales the smoke.

There's plenty of cocaine in Israel, but it's expensive and of poor quality. It passes through so many hands that by the time it reaches Israel it contains less than 10 percent cocaine, and the additives are unhealthy. Coke is known as:

> **kristal** (קריסטל): crystal
>
> **Kristina** (קריסטינה): Christina

tipot af (טיפות אף): nose drops

shura (שורה): a line of coke

Before statehood, the underground organization Lehi, which tried to chase away the British, had a slogan, "From the line [ranks] only death shall free us" (**Meshura yeshchrer rak hamavet** משורה ישחרר רק המוות). This is used today with the meaning of "line" changed to apply to coke or heroin.

To snort any kind of powder is:

lehasnif (להסניף): from the English "sniff"

lehariach (להריח): to smell

lasim ba-af (לשים באף): to put in the nose

Ecstasy is abbreviated to **eksta** (אקסטה) or called **galgalim** (גלגלים), "wheels." It's not as popular as it was in the 1990s, but its active ingredient, MDMA (called simply **em di** אם די), is still very popular. We call it the **sam ahava** (סם אהבה), "love drug," because it makes you feel very sensuous and makes everything look beautiful. A close friend once fell in love so badly while high on MDMA that it took him three months to get rid of the unattractive bimbo.

For those still doing LSD:

trip (טריפ): trip

nesia (נסיעה): journey

karton (קרטון): cardboard, since it usually comes as a soaked piece of cardboard

lelakek kartonim (ללקק קרטונים): to take LSD; literally, "to lick cardboard"

LSD is a bit outdated, but one can still get a weak liquid version of it.

Gat (גת) is a drug you've probably never heard of or know little about. It's the Middle Eastern cousin of the South American coca plant, brought to Israel by Yemenite immigrants. It's chewed for hours, usually with a group of friends, before giving a modest high, which is why it doesn't attract thrill seekers (it's not like snorting a line and getting an instant buzz). In Yemen everything stops in the afternoon, and people take time off to chew—a deeply rooted practice the authorities never succeeded in halting.

The authorities in Israel tried to do the same but didn't succeed either. The mystique of **gat** is its rumored power to enhance libido and cure erectile dysfunction. Very few women do **gat**.

rupta (רופטה): a bundle of **gat** leaves

lechazen (לכאזן): to chew **gat** leaves

tachazina (טכאזינה): a **gat**-chewing party

After you pick the soft leaves, you make a small lump (the size depends on how strong your teeth are), place it in the side of your mouth between your cheeks and molars, chew it to a pulp, and suck the juice out of it. You keep adding leaves and drinking tea or water. The leaves are bitter, so some people add a piece of sugar. After a few hours, you spit the lump out, wash your mouth out, and drink some alcohol. Then you're all set for a pleasant time.

There are two kinds of **gat** plant. The one with reddish stems usually enhances sexual experiences. The one with whitish stems has more poison in it and is unpredictable: it can make you laugh hysterically or weep bitterly; it can make you a superman in bed or a total failure.

While **gat** is mellow, the powder derived from it is quite potent. It's called **chagigat** (חגיגת), a combination of **chagiga** (חגיגה), "party," and **gat**. You can buy **chagigat** at almost any kiosk. It isn't legal but isn't considered as bad as coke. It comes in capsules that can be swallowed, but if you like it through your nose, just open the capsule, release the powder, and sniff it to your heart's delight.

Thugs

When Israel was young, people used to say that once we had homegrown criminals we'd be a normal nation. Well, we got much more than we asked for. Nowadays vicious crime families fight each other with firearms and bombs that occasionally kill innocent bystanders. The situation is especially bad in Netanya (נתניה), a nice vacation town by the sea, south of Tel Aviv, and two old towns east of Tel Aviv: Lod (לוד) and Ramla (רמלה). Netanya is the one place in the world where I don't perform; I don't have what it takes to entertain thugs.

Here's some crime-and-violence lingo:

sanjar (סנג'ר): criminal's apprentice

avaryan tsa-atsua (עבריין צעצוע): petty hoodlum; literally, "a toy criminal"

abaday (אבדאי): thug; literally, "strong"

pushtak (פושטק): ruffian; not a professional criminal, just acts like one

chuligan (חוליגן): same meaning as "hooligan" in English

kepten (קפטן): crime boss; from "captain"

letashesh (לתשש): to steal

lehitlachlech (להתלכלך): to badmouth; literally, "to get dirty"

kafa (כפה): a slap; from **kaf yad** (כף יד), "palm of the hand"

zapta (זפטה): a punch

nogra (נוגרה): A type of assault in which the middle finger, bent out of a fist, strikes the side of the head. It usually leaves a red mark and is done to someone who forgot to do his chores.

bomba (בומבה): a mega-blow

latma (לטמה): a slap dealt for educational reasons

> **Lakach harbe latmot lifney shelamad et luach hakefel**
> (לקח הרבה לטמות לפני שלמד את לוח הכפל): It took a lot of slaps before he learned the multiplication table.

maka yevesha (מכה יבשה): to beat someone severely without leaving marks; usually done by the police; Literally, "a dry blow"

flik (פליק): a slap, usually on the butt for discipline

tchapcha (צ'פחה): a friendly strong pat on the back or the back of the head

lekaseach (לכסח): to break someone's bones

lezayen hatsura (לזיין הצורה): to kick the shit out of someone; literally, "to fuck up someone's shape"

shtinker (שטינקר): informer; from Yiddish

zamir (זמיר): stool pigeon; literally, "nightingale"

mechalel (מחלל): to squeal; also, to give blow jobs, especially in the shower; literally, "to play flute"

levazbez (לבזבז): to waste; euphemism for "to kill"

yatsa letiyul (יצא לטיול): went out for a hike (from which he'll never return)

lishloach zer (לשלוח זר): to get someone killed; literally, "to send a bouquet"

latet ligmor (לתת לגמור): to supply drugs to someone until he drops dead

meter shmonim (מטר שמונים): to put six feet under; literally, "six meters"

manyak (מניאק): a policeman; literally, "a maniac"

tchakalaka (צ'קלאקה): the blue flashing light of a police car

la-asot panim (לעשות פנים): to meet face-to-face to resolve a disagreement; literally, "to make face"

lesacheket kipa aduma (לשחק כיפה אדומה): to trick someone into believing all is well (while planning to harm him); literally, "to play Little Red Riding Hood"

If you buy something or get services with no intention of paying, then you've shopped **al cheshbon habaron** (על חשבון הברון), "on the baron's account," as in Baron Rothschild, who financially supported the small Jewish community in Israel from the late nineteenth century practically until 1948, when the State of Israel was resurrected. Ever since, putting something "on the baron's account" means freeloading. Read more about Rothschild, and the use of his name in slang, in chapter 11.

If asked, "Who is paying for all this?" the traditional answer is, "Schulman will pay" (**schulman yeshalem** שולמן ישלם). Schulman was a legendary professional criminal, a giant of a man, always elegantly dressed and well mannered, but one wrong word turned him into a one-man demolition team. He liked to drink but didn't like to drink alone, so when in a bar, he usually invited everyone for a drink. When the bartender hesitated, he would reply, "Don't worry, Schulman will pay." Needless to say, Schulman never paid.

CHAPTER EIGHT

Army Slang

Israel's mandatory army service is where a lot of colorful slang expressions and jokes originate. Every eighteen-year-old in Israel has to enlist. Men serve for three years and women for two. But the connection to the army doesn't stop there; after compulsory service comes compulsory reserve service. A lot of careers start in the army, especially careers in computer programming.

Until only a few years ago, show business was dominated by artists who got their big break in the army. I'm one of them. As soon as the higher-ups realized I could sing well, I was enlisted as a performer in the Northern Command Entertainment Ensemble. At eighteen I had my first hit. Then came another and another— by the time I left the army I had it made. But I still had to give the army thirty-six days a year, and more than that in times of war. I once spent ninety straight days in Lebanon, doing two or three shows daily. They liked me in the army. I'm self-contained; all I need is my voice and my guitar. And I liked learning new slang, songs, and jokes from the soldiers, which was vital to my career.

One day I came back after a long time abroad, and naturally I called up my army unit to report for duty. I gave my serial number, rank, and name to the unfamiliar young voice that answered the phone. He burst out laughing and said, "Daddy-o, are you still alive?" (**Abale, ata od chay?** ?אבא'לה, אתה עוד חי). He then informed me that I was no longer needed and could come get my discharge papers. You can imagine how I felt about being ingloriously discharged by a young punk after thirty-two years of service. But old soldiers never die. I was mobilized when the next war broke out. Can you now understand the strong ties an Israeli has with his army?

The army is a melting pot in which young people from different backgrounds learn to live with one another. Comradeship tested under fire creates an intimacy a noncombatant can hardly understand. When a soldier says to his comrade, "Your mother sucks Arabs in Gaza" (**Ima shelcha motsetset le-aravim be-aza** אמא שלך מוצצת לערבים בעזה), he is actually saying, "I love you and I know you love me even more than you love your own mother."

In the army, nicknames are usually simple, basic, and descriptive:

masriach (מסריח): stinker

shamen (שמן): fatso

shachor (שחור): black

gamad (גמד): dwarf

kereach (קירח): baldy

The bearers of these nicknames carry them with pride for the rest of their lives and are thrilled to meet an old comrade who yells at them, "Hey, you fucking fatso, does your mother still fuck in the ass?" (**Hey ya shamen mizdayen ima shelcha od ochelet batachatt?** הי יה שמן מזדיין, אמא שלך עוד אוכלת בתחת?).

This strong bond among Israeli men is why they ejaculate so fast; they are in a hurry to run and tell their buddies about their latest conquest.

The army narrows the gap between men and women, and makes for a more equal society. When an Israeli man has had enough and can't take it anymore, he will probably say, "My prick broke down" (**Nishbar li hazayin** נשבר לי הזין). An Israeli woman won't shy away from saying, "My cunt is broken" (**Nishbar li hakus** נשבר לי הכוס).

These slang words and phrases also began their career in the army:

madey alef (מדי א): usually an elegant garment for going out, but in the army it's your regular uniform; literally, "A uniform"

madey bet (מדי ב): usually work or everyday clothes, but in the army it's your battle uniform; literally, "B uniform"

gimelim (גימלים): exemption from chores due to sickness

kitbeg (קיטבג): duffel bag; from "kit bag"

she-elat kitbeg (שאלת קיטבג): a stupid question

When a commander orders his soldiers to stand in formation with their weapons, and then some idiot asks, "With our duffel bags too?" (**Im kitbeg gam?** אם קיטבג גם?), that is a **she-elat kitbeg**, and the commander usually replies with a sarcastic **ken** (כן), "yes."

nikur (ניקור): sleeping while on duty; literally, "pecking"

jobnik (ג'ובניק): noncombatant soldier; from the English word "job"

ptsatsa (פצצה): an extremely beautiful girl; literally, "bomb"

A girl with a pretty face and an awful body is described in combat terminology as having **partsuf ptsatsa, guf kmo achrey haptsatsa** (פרצוף פצצה, גוף כמו אחרי הפצצה): "a face like a bomb, but a body like after a bombardment." A dazzling girl is a **ptsatsot lagabot** (פצצות לגבות), which literally means "bombs to the eyebrows."

lehitchaber lavrid (להתחבר לווריד): to bother relentlessly; literally, "to get attached to the vein"

Hu yoshen im dargot al hapidjama.

mural (מורעל): a soldier who loves serving in the army; literally, "poisoned"

Hu yoshen im dargot al hapidjama, ad kdey kach hu mural al hatsava

(הוא ישן עם דרגות על הפיז'מה, עד כדי כך הוא מורעל על הצבא): He sleeps with ranks on his pajamas; that's how poisoned he is by the army.

sarut bamoach (שרוט במוח): crazy; literally, "scratched in the head"

lehachzir tsiyud (להחזיר ציוד): to drop dead; literally, "to return your gear," which is what soldiers do when they end their service

Shortcuts and adaptations

The army loves contractions and acronyms because they're effi-
cient. It also likes to use one word to describe an emotion or
event that usually takes many words. Some of these slang abbre-
viations and adaptations originated in the army:

zabasho (זבשו): that's his problem; contracted from **zu
habeaya shelo** (זו הבעייה שלו)

pizdeloch (פיזדלוך): remote place; a combination of the
Romanian word *pizda,* "pussy," and the Yiddish *loch,* "hole"

chamshush (חמשוש): weekend leave; contracted from the
words for Thursday and Friday, **chamishi** (חמישי) and **shishi**
(יום שישי), respectively

helmut (הלמוט): one who has shell shock; from **helem** (הלם),
"shock"

zubur (זובור): initiation ceremony in which veteran soldiers
haze the new guys; from **zubi**

regila (רגילה): regular leave; literally, "regular"

smicha (שמיכה): Blanket. When a soldier deserves a good
ass-kicking, his comrades put a blanket over him, so he can't
see his assailants, and proceed to kick the shit out of him.

The dark side

A soldier is sure to have a brush with death during his time in
the army. Not surprisingly, this has bred quite a bit of gallows
humor. There is a saying, "A soldier who hasn't experienced jail

is no real soldier" (**Chayal shelo haya bakele eyno chayal amiti** חייל שלא היה בכלא אינו חייל אמיתי). I was a real soldier and one time when I was sent to cool off in what is called a **beyt havra-ah** (בית הבראה), or "military convalescent home," I saw written on my cell wall in brown letters, with actual shit, "Death is worth committing suicide" (**Mavet shave hitabdut** מוות שווה התאבדות).

Every war, and there have been quite a few, yields at least one macabre song like the one we sang during the 1982 Lebanon War that went: **Anachnu shneynu meota sakit / Girdu et shneynu beota kapit** (אנחנו שנינו מאותה שקית / גרדו את שנינו באותה כפית), "From the same body bag we are / Scooped by the same spoon into the same jar."

No wonder the word **tamut** (תמות), "drop dead," is used for practically every occasion. From this same Israeli dark side comes the slang word for a nerd, **sabon** (סבון): literally, "soap." Few Israelis know its origin. When the Holocaust survivors, mostly Eastern European Jews, arrived in Israel, they were considered nerdier than their Middle Eastern counterparts and were nicknamed **sabon** because the Nazis used to make soap out of their victims' body fat.

CHAPTER NINE

Words from All Over

Regional

Israel is a small country, and most of its slang originates in the metropolis of Tel Aviv, the Big Orange (**Hatapuz Hagadol** התפוז הגדול). However, many other cities have their own vernaculars, which include both words distinct to the region and others that migrate.

Be'er Sheva (באר שבע) / Beersheba

Be'er Sheva, at the heart of the Negev desert region, is about six thousand years old and houses a colorful bedouin market, a university, and the legendary Abraham's Well. **Raban** (רבן), the Sephardic word for "rabbi," is the most sophisticated slang word and is specific to that region. Out of this three-letter word, Beershebans can create any term they might conceivably need.

For example, this sentence was addressed to me by a friend from Beersheba: **Bo nelech kodem laraban, nitraben lo**

**al hahitrabnut shelo, venelech larabanit, haraban shela
mitrraben becul, hi ohevet lehitraben, neraben ota venitra-
ben aleha** (‫בא נלך לרבן, נתרבן לו על ההתרבנות שלו, ונלך לרבנית, הרבן‬
‫ ;(שלה מתתרבן בחו'ל, היא אוהבת להתרבן, נרבן אותה ונתרבן עליה‬that is,
"First let's go to the dude (**raban**), hustle him (**nitraben**) out of
his drugs (**hitrabnut**), and then go to the chick (**rabanit**), while
her husband is enjoying (**mitraben**) himself abroad; she likes to
get high (**lehitraben**), so we'll get her high (**neraben**) and screw
(**nitraben**) her."

Gi'vatayim (‫גבעתים‬)

A sleepy working-class satellite of Tel Aviv, Gi'vatayim is known
for its own excessively used word. Not as sophisticated as **raban**,
since you can't use it as a verb, it's widely applied as the equivalent of "dude" or "girl."

Masculine, Feminine

singular

urdun (‫אורדון‬), **urdunit** (‫אורדונית‬)

plural

urdunim (‫אורדונים‬), **urduniyot** (‫אורדוניות‬)

When referring to a third party, **hey** (‫ה‬) is added as a prefix:
for example, **haurdun** (‫האורדון‬), "the dude," or **haurduniyot**
(‫האורדוניות‬), "the girls." No matter where they meet, whether in
Tel Aviv or in the Sahara, dudes from Gi'vatayim will always
cheerfully call out to each other, "Hey, **urdun**, what's up?" (**Hey
urdun, ma hamatsav?** ‫הי אורדון, מה המצב?‬). The title is an honor

for an outsider—I remember my elation when an acquaintance officially made me a bosom buddy by greeting me with it.

This word can also be applied to places such as coffeehouses, clubs, and restaurants. In this case **ya** (יה) is added at the end: **urduniya** (אורדונייה). You might hear the sentence **Hey urdun, bo nikach et haurduniyot venelech laurduniya, gam haurdun yihiye sham** (היי אורדון, בוא ניקח את האורדוניות ונלך לאורדונייה, גם האורדון יהיה שם): "Hey, buddy (**urdun**), let's take the girls (**urduniyot**) and go to the club (**urduniya**)—our friend (**haurdun**) will also be there."

Haifa (חיפה)

Haifa has splendid beaches and magnificent views from Mount Carmel, the site of the golden-domed Baha'i Shrine and Gardens. Aside from being a holy place for people of the Baha'i faith, Haifa is also home to the most attractive boys and girls in Israel. This abundance of hotness leads to exceptional amounts of sex. So **nosim lechaifa** (נוסעים לחיפה), "going to Haifa," has come to mean "having sex."

An Israeli girl will know exactly what you have in mind if you say **Ma da-atech shenelech elay umisham nisa lechaifa?** (מה דעתך שנלך אלי ומשם ניסע לחיפה?): "What do you say we go to my place and from there we go to Haifa?"

Rehovot (רחובות)

This city twenty miles from Tel Aviv was established in 1890 by Polish Jews and later attracted Yemenite Jews, who planted orange groves and vineyards. Today it's mainly known for the Weizmann Institute of Science.

Most of the slang used in Rehovot is outdated, but the city

has been the source of some useful words for articles of clothing, such as **pokras** (פוקרס) for a long-sleeved T-shirt. God only knows how this very useful word developed.

Anpilaot (האנפילאות), "slippers," is a word used in the Talmud. The current term is **na-aley bayit** (נעלי בית), but using the archaic form is definitely cool in the right situation. You'll get a laugh, for instance, if you see a pretty young girl with a pair of new designer shoes and ask her, **Me-efo ha-anpilaot haelu?** (?מאיפה האנפילאות האלו): "Where'd you get those slippers?"

Yerushalayim (ירושלים) / Jerusalem

The three monotheistic religions hold Jerusalem sacred, and two consider it to be the navel of the world. When I'm there, I always have a feeling that God is watching over my shoulder, and it's hard to have a good time. But wherever there is holiness, the Black Dog is present to taint it and lure people's souls into dark places. There's plenty of nightlife and sleaze to be found. Nevertheless, when the denizens of Jerusalem feel the urge to have a jolly old time, they usually go to Tel Aviv, which is only forty miles away.

Jerusalem slang is as archaic as it gets. Take, for instance, the Hebrew word for a Frenchman, **farangi** (פראנג'י). In AD 1099, when the inhabitants of the Holy City first beheld the predominantly French crusaders, they were very impressed by their elegant garments. Though outdated, **farangi** is still in use all over Israel to designate a dandy or someone dressing in that style.

Even older than **farangi** is **chapachula** (צ'פאצ'ולה), a term used for a simple, not too bright, not too pretty girl. It comes from the Greek word *chapachulis* meaning "a wet and dirty person." Alexander the Great conquered Jerusalem in 332 BC, and the Hellenes ruled Israel until 140 BC, when the Jews whooped

their asses. But by then they had already left their cultural mark on the city—this Greek word still rules.

Ma ata mitlabesh farangi kaze lapgisha im hachapach-ula hazot? (?מה אתה מתלבש פראנג'י כזה לפגישה עם הצ'פאצ'ולה הזאת): "Why do you dress up so elegantly (**farangi**) for a date with that ugly chick (**chapachula**)?"

Tel Aviv (תֵּל־אָבִיב): "Spring Mound"

Theodor Herzl, an Austrian Jew, founded Zionism not as an ideology but as the pragmatic solution to the acute Jewish problem in the late nineteenth century. He envisioned "a place where Jews can grow their noses as long as they please to their hearts' delight." The original German title of his utopian book describing the ideal state was *Alteneuland*, which means "old-new land." The founding fathers wanted to give the first modern Israeli city that name, but it didn't really work. Menachem Sheinkin (for whom the hippest street in the city is named) came up with a brilliant solution: **Tel**, literally, "an archeological mound" and **Aviv**, "spring," suggesting at once old and new.

Tel Aviv has many sobriquets. I've already mentioned the Big Orange, which may have come from the Big Apple. A 24-7 kind of town, Tel Aviv is known, New York–style, as "the city without pause" (**ir lelo hafsaka** עיר ללא הפסקה).

It's also sometimes called **medinat Tel Aviv** (מדינת תל אביב), "the state of Tel Aviv," because Tel Aviv isn't really Israel any more than New York City is the United States. It's a cosmopolitan sphere with a culture of its own. No matter what happens in the rest of Israel—war or flood—life as Tel Avivans know it will go on as usual.

The name **habua** (הבועה), "the bubble," came into use when southern Israel was showered with missiles, driving its inhabitants into shelters, while the party continued in Tel Aviv. **Habua** now refers to a core group of young people, mostly out-of-towners, who dedicate their energy to looking for the most decadent fun, the hottest gossip, and the latest fashion. The city's inner circle, they vie to come up with the best new and bizarre slang—words and phrases that hardly ever leave the bubble.

Tel Aviv is also called **ir hachataim** (עיר החטאים), "sin city," but mostly by nonresidents. To the Tel Avivan, it's **ir habiluyim** (עיר הבילויים), "fun city."

It's hard to identify much slang as uniquely Tel Avivan, since whatever is coined there quickly becomes the slang of all Israel. Here is some slang that's current on the street:

> **piguz** (פיגוז): very nice or very good; literally, "bombing"

> **Hakol tost** (הכל טוסט): Everything is good. Literally, "Everything is toast." Wordplay on **Hakol tov** (הכל טוב), "Everything is good," the conventional answer to "How do you do?"

> **lichyot beseret** (לחיות בסרט): to live in a movie; i.e., vaguely connected to reality

> **makati** (מכתי): pest

> **lehitalyen** (להתעליין): to talk down to people

> **lehitkaten** (להתקטן): to be petty; from **katan** (קטן), "small"

> **lachpor** (לחפור): nag and nag; literally, "to dig"

> **bulbuli** (בולבולי): my dick

This last innocent and unsexual term, based on **bulbul,** one of many Hebrew names for the penis, is vying to replace the popular **achi** (my brother) as a greeting. I came back to the country, after being away for just a few months, and found people addressing one another as "my dick"!

stam (סתם): just joking; usually drawn out, **staaaaaaaaamm** (סתאאאאאם)

Kibbutzim (קיבוצים)

At the beginning of the twentieth century, starry-eyed young Jews, dreaming of a new, just world, immigrated to Israel from czarist Russia. They hoped to bring their revolutionary ideas to life in their ancient homeland, at the time a malaria-ridden, remote part of the decaying Ottoman Empire. These **chalutsim** (חלוצים), "pioneers," founded the famous collectives known as kibbutzim, a pure form of communism that's now outlived the USSR by a number of years.

This special style of living required quite a bit of new vocabulary. Here are some terms that are still in use:

chaver (חבר): comrade

hashkava (השכבה): Putting to bed. This nightly ritual involves parents taking their kids to the dormitory where all kibbutz kids sleep, then showering in unisex communal showers and going to bed themselves in a tiny, bare-bones room; that is, if there is no obligatory meeting in the communal dining room to discuss some pressing ideological matter.

kolboynik (כלבוייניק): a bowl for garbage found on each of the dining tables; literally, "everything in it"

daysa (דייסה): any warm side dish; literally, "porridge"

salat chamorim (סלט חמורים): donkey's salad, a mix of vegetables crudely chopped in no-frills Bolshevik style

lebeniya (לבנייה): skimmed buttermilk

> The kibbutzniks call rich, spoiled city kids **yaldey shament** (ילדי שמנת), "sour cream kids," and city kids call young kibbutzniks **yaldey lebeniya** (ילדי לבנייה), "skimmed buttermilk kids."

sukarya borachat (סוכרייה בורחת): Literally, "a candy that runs away." Or so it seems to the kids who first spot and try to grab these jellies that are sometimes served when the kibbutz splurges on a festive dinner for a special holiday.

komuna (קומונה): The laundry storeroom where comrades bring their dirty laundry and pick up a clean set of clothes by size. There is no private ownership, not even of clothing. Literally, "commune."

sheat ahava (שעת אהבה): love hour, the half hour (around noon) parents spend with their children

primus (פרימוס): a single person living together with a couple in one tiny room

Roots

English

Because the territory that's now Israel was a British colony from World War I until 1948, some English-flavored slang lingers on. Much of it is military (Israelis served in the British army during World War II) or automotive (the British were the first to export cars to Israel).

pancher (פנצ׳ר): flat tire; from "puncture"

after (אפטר): a short leave; from the few hours of free time a soldier gets after duty, when his chores are done

Ani gomer la-avod mukdam hayom, efshar la-alot elay-ich leafter? (אני גומר לעבוד מוקדם היום, אפשר לעלות אליך לאפטר?): I finish work early today; can I come up and see you for an **after**?

mesting (מסטינג): Originally, this referred to two square bowls made out of aluminum that fit one in the other and were used by soldiers in the British army for food and drink (from the English "mess tin"); now it's a rich metaphor. No Hebrew phrase expresses a deeper bond than **le-echol meoto hamesting** (לאכול מאותו המסטינג), "to eat out of the same mess tin." A smart woman won't tell her husband that he has to choose between her and his unmarried buddy, because there's a big chance he'll say **At yoda-at, achalnu meoto mesting** (אתה יודע אכלנו מאותו מסטינג): "You know we ate out of the same mess tin."

When you run into someone three times in a row over a short period of time, you can say, "A third-time ice cream" (**Pa-am shlishit glida** פעם שלישית גלידה). Or just, "Buy me an ice cream" (**Tikne li glida** תקנה לי גלידה). Since I was a child, I wondered what seeing someone for the third time had to do with ice cream. Turns out the phrase dates back to the British Mandate and is a corruption of the English sentence "If I see you a third time, I'll scream."

The word **mandatory** (מנדטורי) is slang meaning "outdated"; i.e., from the British Mandate.

Turkish

From the thirteenth century to World War I, Israel was part of the
vast Ottoman Empire. So if you want to suggest that something
is even more ancient or passé than **mandatory** suggests, use the
slang word **otomany** (עותומאני). The Turkish influence persists in
a few other phrases:

> **chuzuk** (חוזוק): a harsh beating; from a thin stick used for
> torture
>
> > **Ani lo rotse lisgor et haor o havilon veim tamshich
> > lehatsits lechadar hasheyna sheli tekabel mimeni
> > chuzuk shelo tishkac** (אני לא רוצה לסגור את האור או הווילון
> > ואם לא תפסיק להציץ לי לחדר השינה תקבל ממני חוזוק שלא תשכח):
> > I don't want to shut off the light or close the curtains, and
> > if you keep on peeping into my bedroom, you'll get a
> > **chuzuk** you won't forget.
>
> **charman** (חרמן): horny, a craving for drugs
>
> **metchukmak** (מצ׳וקמק): shriveled
>
> > **Al tagid li sheata rotse lezayen oti im hadavar
> > hamechukmak haze** (אל תגיד לי שאתה רוצה לזיין אותי עם
> > הדבר המצ׳וקמק הזה): Don't tell me you want to fuck me
> > with that shriveled thing of yours.

Yiddish

At its height about a century ago, Yiddish was the everyday
language of more than ten million people worldwide. That was
before extermination and assimilation took their toll. David Ben-
Gurion, the first Israeli prime minister, was raised on Yiddish

but came to see it as a ghetto language, a sign of the Diaspora, and tried to stop its use. As a child, I was terribly embarrassed whenever my mother spoke Yiddish in front of my friends, yet this resourceful, vivid, witty language lives on in present-day Israeli culture.

Here are some very current slang words of Yiddish origin:

tarante (טרנטה): jalopy, used for anything old (I used it for my old dog in chapter 3)

Ani lo mekayem yoter yechasim im hazkena sheli, hi kvar tarante (אני לא מקיים יותר יחסים עם הזקנה שלי, היא כבר טרנטה): I don't have sex with my old lady anymore; she's already a jalopy.

klafte (קלפטה): a bitch and a witch in one

lefargen (לפרגן): to look favorably on someone's success, to wish well, to be sympathetic

Grushati chaya achshav im mishehu vehi meod meusheret veani mefargen la acharey kol ma sheavra iti (גרושתי חייה עכשיו עם מישהו והיא מאוד מאושרת ואני מפרגן לה אחרי כל מה שעברה איתי): My ex-wife is living with somebody now and is very happy; after what she went through with me, I wish her well.

Arabic

Israel owes a lot to multilayered, gloriously obscene Arabic curses. One marvelous phrase we've appropriated is **kus ocht abuk ars** (כוס אוחת אבוק ערס), "the pussy of the sister of your father the pimp." Though this curse attacks the father, the final target is his sister's cunt—a theme in Arabic swearing. This is heavy stuff: it curses the whole family. Save it for when you're really pissed off.

in-al abuk (אינעל אבוק): holy shit

> **In-al abuk ech noda la sheani nasuy?**
> (?אינעל אבוק איך נודע לה שאני נשוי): Holy shit! How did she find out I was married?

Sababi and Rhyming

Taken from Arabic, the word **sababa** (סבבה) means "groovy" in Hebrew. At some point **sababa** evolved into **sababi** (סבבי), simply because it sounds better and is easier to pronounce. Then **babi** (no meaning) was added for its rhyming effect and the term became **sababi babi** (סבבי בבי).

You can tell a person's mood by the version of **sababa** he uses.

sababa: bad to fair mood

sababi: fair to good mood

sababi babi: good to excellent mood

Israelis love rhyming phrases. Another word that comes from Arabic is **ach-la** (אחלה), which means "awesome." If you add a meaningless **bachla** to it, you get **achla bachla** (אחלה בחלה), very awesome.

(You can also emphasize a word by simply repeating it. When you want to describe someone really stupid, you say he's an **idiot idiot** (אדיוט אדיוט). **Idiot** means the same in Hebrew as in English.

Russian

At the beginning of last century, Russian Jews were dominant in Israel. They strictly spoke Hebrew, or at least they tried. It was hard to revive a language that had been dormant for two thousand years, its terminology fit for a world long gone. But they did their best, inventing new words for modern appliances and situations: for instance, **schak-rachok** (שחק-רחק), literally, "distance speaker," for the telephone.

Many of these words are obsolete but some Russian-Hebrew curses have endured. The most popular for a long time was **kibinimat** (קיבינימט), "your mother's cunt." It has evolved and now means "a godforsaken place." If you're stuck in a dumpy hostel on the outskirts of town, you can say **Ani mitareach be-eyze makom bekibinimat** (אני מתארח באיזה מקום בקיבינימט): "I'm staying in some godforsaken place." People will know what you mean and may invite you to stay with them.

More Russian-rooted words that are used as Hebrew slang:

cholera (חולרע): badass motherfucker

barr-dakk (ברדק): whorehouse, a complete mess

ballaggan (בלגן): tumult, mayhem

chall-toorra (חלטורה): a shoestring operation

Your mother's global cunt

Our ethnic versatility allows us to swear in many languages. Take the mother of all curses, "your mother's cunt." In addition to the Russian-derived **kibinimat**, you can take your pick among:

kus emak (כוס אמק): Arabic

pitchka da maikata (פיצ'קה דמייקטה): Bulgarian

tabun emak (טבון אמק): Moroccan

pizda mati (פיזדה מטי): Romanian

These are all in use to some degree, but the Arabic phrase prevails. It is the most common and basic Israeli swearword, used excessively for every occasion. Uttered almost automatically by Israelis, its meaning shifts with the situation and the intonation. It can mean "not on your life" or "fuck you," and it can even express enthusiasm: **Kus emak, tistakel al habachura hayafa hazu!** (כוס אמק, תסתכל על הבחורה היפה הזו!): "Motherfucker, look at that pretty girl!"

A friend of mine used to be a big shot in an important company. **Kus emak** was so strongly embedded in his vocabulary that he used it in every other sentence. There were complaints from people he worked with. His superiors warned him, but he couldn't shake **kus emak** from his system. Now my unemployed friend has a good reason to swear.

CHAPTER TEN

Wired

Israel is a high-tech place. Research labs abound and gadgets sell big. Techie terminology is mostly composed of English words lightly adapted to sound like Hebrew.

Fakatsit

Young adolescent girls known as **fakatsot** (פקצות), or **fakatsa** (פקצה) in the singular, are creating a unique and fast-spreading Internet slang called **fakatsit** (פקצית). The word **fakatsa**, originally an army designation meaning "military secretary," has had many meanings but now seems to have landed on these preteens and teens who rule the Net.

The **fakatsot** are also called **metsachtsechot shinayim** (מצחצחות שיניים), "toothbrushers," because their blogs are typically full of trivial information along the lines of **Kamti baboker vetsichtsachti shinayim** (קמתי בבוקר וצחצחתי שיניים): "Woke up in the morning and brushed my teeth."

fakatsa

Their Web sites favor the color pink and the kitsch Japanese style known as *kawaii*, reflecting the **fakatsot** affinity for the Far Eastern subculture of young girls with a strong consumer instinct. Many of these blogs declare, "Love *kawaii*" (**ohevet kaway** אוהבת קוואי).

A few years ago, a Motorola commercial featured someone saying "Moshi moshi," a Japanese telephone greeting. *Moshi* sounds like an abbreviation of the Hebrew word **mushlam** (מושלם), which means "perfect." Now the **fakatsot** say **moshi-moshi** (מושי-מושי), "perfect perfect," all the time.

Another cultural influence is South American TV, especially Argentine soap operas, which leads to wide use of Spanish words in the blogs.

> **muy** (מוי): very
>
> **mucho** (מוצ׳ו): much
>
> **obvio** (אוביו): obvious

Their third source of inspiration is, of course, American youth. They like Bratz dolls, Paris Hilton, and Britney Spears. They say "like, duh" in English or "LOL" instead of the traditional Hebrew **chhhh** (חחחחח), the onomatopoeic word for Israeli laughter.

Hebrew is resilient enough to absorb some English Internet terms:

> **lelankek** (ללנקק): to use a link; literally, "to link around"
>
> **leatetch** (לאטץ): to attach
>
> **tokbekistim** (טוקבקיסטים): comment makers; literally, "talk-backers"
>
> **letakbek** (לתקבק): to comment

Their world may seem trivial and their writing casual, with a lot of exclamation marks, but these young girls have tons of influence on Internet surfers, who use much of their slang. Thanks to them, you don't necessarily need Hebrew letters on your keyboard to type in Hebrew; you can use their alphabet, **fakatsit** (same name as the language).

The Fakatsit Alphabet

Hebrew letter	Roman alphabet equivalent	slang letter
א	a	% or K or X
ב	b	2
ג	g	t
ד	d	T
ו	v, w	1 or !
ח	ch	n
ט	t	6
י	y, i, e	^ or *
כ	c	c or >
ל	l	5
מ	m	N
נ	n	]
ס	s	0 or o or @
ע	a	y

Hebrew letter	Roman alphabet equivalent	slang letter
פ	p, f	9
צ	ts	3
ר	r	7
ש	sh	w
ת	t	- ^

This slang alphabet comes in handy when there is no Hebrew lettering on a keyboard, which is everywhere outside Israel. Here is an example of how to use it.

Take the word **tayar** (תייר), "tourist." In **fakatsit** the four-letter Hebrew word is reduced to three letters because one is unpronounced: **tyr** (תיר). Now look up the corresponding Hebrew letters or their roman-alphabet equivalents on the chart above, and you'll see that in **fakatsit** the word can be spelled **7*- ^.**

Here are some phrases commonly translated into **fakatsit**, along with equivalent shorthand signs that are used like emoticons. The middle column shows fakatsa-speak, which is how fakatsas usually type words when not using signs.

English	fakatsa-speak	fakatsit sign
What the fuck?!	ווהט דה פאאאק ?!"""*	0=
Like, duh!	כאילו דה???	$=
Stunning!	מדהים!!!!	((=
Rules!	שולטת!!!!!	8=
Like, people!	לייק,,, פיפול!!! `	@-
Awesome!	מוש!!! * W1N	&:
Ha ha ha, funny!	חחחחחח* סה מסחיק*!!!	CD
What a sexy guy!	סה כ!ol'	@}=
What a sexy girl!	סה קוסעע'	@=
How cute!	סה מ!ש!!!'	(((=
What?!	N סהo?!?	[]=
My dear . . .	נשמאאמי!!	!=
What's up?	מה [???ש*]	^=
I'm dyingggg!	אני מתהההה!	/=
Excuse me?!	סl*-n ההה?!?	()()()=
Fuck offfff!	סה מפו@$#!!!!	# =
For real?	במת?	<>=

Israeli youth have begun to use the **fakatsit** letters even when a Hebrew keyboard is around.

yadayim ktsarot

CHAPTER ELEVEN

Money Is Not All— It's First of All

Israel's economy withstood the financial crisis of 2008 much better than bigger, older economies. If you intend to do business in Israel, here are some words and phrases you should know.

Kesef ze lo hakol, ze kodem kol (כסף זה לא הכל, זה קודם כל): Money is not all—it's first of all.

bunker (בונקר): where a frugal person keeps his money

bunkerist (בונקריסט): a frugal person (masculine)

bunkeristit (בונקריסטית): a frugal person (feminine)

eyn lo grush al hatachat (אין לו גרוש על התחת): without a penny to his name; literally, "without a penny on his ass"

> **Hu medaber al asakim shel milyonim aval bentayim eyn lo grush al hatachat**
> (הוא מדבר על עסקים במיליונים אבל בינתיים אין לו גרוש על התחת): He talks about business in the millions; meanwhile doesn't have a penny on his ass.

kisim amukim (כיסים עמוקים): deep pockets

lasim yad bakis (לשים יד בכיס): to spend money; literally, "to put a hand in the pocket"

yadayim ktsarot (ידיים קצרות): a miser; literally, "short hands" (which can't reach one's pocket)

onat hamelafefonim (עונת המלפפנים): period when there is no business; literally, "cucumber season," which means "silly season"

bakshish (בקשיש): bribe, freebie; from the Turkish

lehafsid et hamichnasayim (להפסיד את המכנסיים): to go broke; literally, "to lose one's pants"

luftgesheften (לופטגשפטן): speculation with no real substance; literally, "air business"

lidfok kupa (לדפוק קופה): to profit, to make a financial killing

lo tov, lo kesef (לא טוב, לא כסף): If you don't like it, you'll get your money back. Literally, "no good, no money." This expression is popular with salesmen.

mocher lokshim (מוכר לוקשים): selling lies; literally, "selling noodles"

juba (ג'ובה): any currency; **jubot** (ג'ובות)

lesachek partya (לשחק פרטייה): swindle

lira levana leyom shachor (לירה לבנה ליום שחור): put aside for hard times; literally, "a white lira for a black day" (lira is an old Israeli currency)

stifa (סטיפה): a large sum of money

milim kmo chol veyn ma le-echol (מילים כמו חול ואין מה לאכול):
endless talking and no business; literally, "words plentiful as
sand and nothing to eat"

kombina (קומבינה): a scheme, a plot; literally, "a combination"

ze lo esek (זה לא עסק): it's not good business; literally, "it's
no business"

> **Ze lo esek liknot beyoker velimkor bezol**
> (זה לא עסק לקנות ביוקר ולמכור בזול): It's not good business to
> buy expensive and sell cheap.

Watch out for businessmen that say **yihiye beseder** (יהיה בסדר),
"it will be okay," or **smoch** (סמוך) "count on me" (literally, "count").

The Rothschilds

The Rothschild family has played a crucial role in world economy
for the last two hundred years. Dynasty founder Mayer Amschel
Rothschild certainly knew opportunity when it knocked, but integ-
rity was the bedrock of his fortune. In 1806, when Napoléon was
about to take Frankfurt, its ruler, William IX, landgrave of Hesse-
Cassel, fled to Denmark, leaving his treasures under the protec-
tion of the Rothschilds. The canny Mayer hid all the jewels, gold,
silverware, and banknotes. And no matter how harshly the French
interrogated him and his family, no one talked. Many turbulent
years later, William, was astounded to find that the Rothschilds
had not only safeguarded his treasures but invested his money at a
good profit. This success propelled the Rothschilds' ascent.

My late father, may his soul rest in peace, urged Mayer's ethos
on me. I must have been a great disappointment to him. He was

Lama ata mashir et haor ba-ambatya,
ata choshev sheani rotshild?

an excellent businessman and, before immigrating to Israel, a star goalie in the legendary Jewish soccer team Hakoah Vienna. To his chagrin, I was more interested in books, girls, and the violin. When I inherited the family business, I made a mess of it; but I will never forget the echo of the Rothschilds that came from his deathbed: "Always make sure the people you deal with are happy with the deal" (**D-ag tamid shelu imam ate ose asakim yihyu merutsim mehaiska** דאג תמיד שאלו עימם אתה עושה עסקים יהיו מרוצים מהעסקה).

> **rotshild** (רוטשילד): beyond rich
>
> **Lama ata mashir et haor ba-ambatya, ata choshev sheani rotshild?**
>
> (למה אתה משאיר את האור באמבטיה, אתה חושב שאני רוטשילד?)
> Why are you leaving the light on in the bathroom—do you think I'm a Rothschild?

When the musical *Fiddler on the Roof* was translated into Hebrew, the words to the song "If I Were a Rich Man" became, "If I were a Rothschild, hy di didl" (**Lu hayiti rotshild, hai di didl** לו הייתי רוטשילד, היי די דידל).

Rothschild didn't get to be so rich just by being trustworthy. He was also a solid businessman, even as a child. As legend has it, young Crown Prince William (before he became landgrave) came to the ghetto to check on his Jewish subjects. He saw a group of children playing and threw a handful of coins to them. The children happily scrambled, grabbing for the coins. Rothschild, however, demanded the coins from the other kids and handed them back to the bewildered prince, saying, "Thank you, but we are not beggars." The crown prince was impressed and asked Rothschild to show him around the ghetto. At the end of the tour, when he was just about to take his leave, Rothschild asked the crown prince to pay him for serving as his guide.

Terms You Should Know

A

Attention seeking: **tsumi** (צומי)

Asshole: **naknik** (נקניק)

B

Buddy: **urdun** (אורדון)

Bimbo: **frecha** (פרחה)

Berserk: **janan** (ג'ננה)

Blunder: **fashla** (פאשלה)

Bend someone's ear: **lebalbel et habeytsim** (לבלבל את הביצים)

C

Chastise: **latet barosh** (לתת בראש)

Confusion: **balbala** (בלבלה)

Charge (money): **lecharger** (לצ'רג'ר)

Crazy: **srita bamoach** (סריטה במוח)

Cravings: **duda** (דודה)

Come (v.): **ligmor** (לגמור)

D

Depressed: **diki** (דיכי)

Dumb (stupid): **satum** (סתום)

Daddy-o: **abale** (אבא'לה)

Drive (someone) crazy: **lehavi et hachalastra** (להביא את החלסטרה)

Dirty mouth: **pe jora** (פה ג'ורה)

E

Exactly: **fix** (פיקס)

F

Flow (v.): **lizrom** (לזרום)

Fucked-up: **dafuk** (דפוק)

Foe: **tchilba** (צ'ילבה)

Fun: **kef** (כיף)

G

Good-looking dame: **shasi** (שסי)

Go to hell: **lech leaza** (לך לעזה)

Groovy: **sababa** (סבבה)

Get lost: **lech tizdayen** (לך תזדיין)

H

High (drug induced): **sutul** (סוטול)

Hanky-panky: **putchi mutchi** (פוצ'י מוצ'י)

Horny: **charman** (חרמן)

I

Idiot: **chamor** (חמור)

In short . . . : **uktsur** (אוקצור)

J

Joint (pot): **tsingale** (צינגלה)

Jinx: **nachs** (נאחס)

K

Kick ass: **lekaseach** (לכסח)

L

Live in la-la land: **lichyot beseret** (לחיות בסרט)

Leave someone standing: **lehavriz** (להבריז)

Lucky: **mazalitiko** (מזליטיקו)

M

Mayhem: **karachana** (קרחנה)

Money: **jubot** (ג'ובות)

N

Nonsense: **kishkush** (קשקוש)

Nerd: **laflaf** (לפלף) or **chnun** (חנון) or **yoram** (יורם) or **sabon** (סבון)

Nag: **lachpor** (לחפור)

O

One-night stand: **stuts** (סטוץ)

P

Pain in the ass: **makati** (מכתי)

Piece of cake: **lehavi behalicha** (להביא בהליכה)

Pull someone's leg: **avoda baeynayim** (עבודה בעיניים)

Pissed off: **mevoas** (מבואס)

Q

Quickie: **chafuz** (חפוז)

R

Religious: **dos** (דוס)

S

Sublime: **sof haderech** (סוף הדרך)

Son of a bitch: **ben zona** (בן זונה)

Swallows (come): **bola-at** (בולעת)

Stoned: **mastul** (מסטול)

Spectacular: **betseva** (בצבע)

Stash: **zula** (זולה)

Slap: **kafa** (כפה)

U

Urination: **likshor et hachamor** (לקשור את החמור)

V

Vagabond: **archi-parchi** (ארחי פרחי)

W

Wait in vain: **lehityabesh** (להתייבש)

Y

Yuck: **ichs** (איכס)

Z

Zealous: **mashkian** (משקיען)